D0922515

BEING & VIBRATION

BEING &
VIBRATION

by Joseph Rael

WITH MARY ELIZABETH MARLOW

COUNCIL OAK BOOKS

Council Oak Books, LLC
1615 South Baltimore, Suite 3
Tulsa, Oklahoma 74119

BEING AND VIBRATION

Book design by Carol Haralson
Cover art © Nicholas Wilson
Cover design by Michele Wetherbee

Library of Congress Card Catalog Number
92-72320

Printed in the United States of America

02 03 04 05   5 4 3 2 1

CONTENTS

Also by Joseph Rael
Beautiful Painted Arrow

Also by Mary Elizabeth Marlow
Handbook for the Emerging Woman

INTRODUCTION

*S*ome meetings are Divine Appointments. Such, I believe, was the case with my meeting with Beautiful Painted Arrow (Joseph Rael) some ten years ago. Joseph had come to Virginia Beach to teach a weekend seminar. I remember taking a solitary walk down a path in the woods and stopping dead-still when Joseph approached coming from the opposite direction. We looked intently at each other. It was a sacred moment. There were no words spoken, yet there was a great deal communicated. Inside him was deep peace. One thing I knew, this man is a keeper of the ancient wisdom. Here is the soul of a mystic, one who has merged with the heart of God.

It took five years for our paths to cross again. I had just returned from India, culminating a seventeen year exploration in Eastern thought, with a sense that it was now time to immerse myself in the mysticism of my own land. As if on cue, Joseph reappeared in my life. With little need for re-introductions, we began teaching seminars and retreat programs together. Joseph impacts those around him on a multitude of levels. Whenever I am in his presence, there is the sense of automatically being shifted up an octave to a higher level of awareness, so I found myself learning from him, often without any conscious effort on my part.

This has become my greatest adventure, one which has catapulted me into experiences which heretofore I would have considered miraculous. Now I view them as a natural part of what happens when one is moved to a higher octave of vibration.

Any confusion over seemingly conflicting forms from various traditions soon faded. I quickly grew to honor the Native American tradition in which Joseph is rooted and to understand both the value of form and the paradox of not getting "stuck in the form," (as Joseph often says) for ultimately all form must be transcended. Though Joseph is Native American, his vision is not limited to one tradition or one philosophy. It comes from a resonating vibration which lifts us to a level of consciousness beyond form, a place where we discover our own myth-making ability.

Writing a book with Joseph has been an adventure of another kind, a profound myth-making process. The time we spent working on the book together could be defined as extended time, a vibration where there is no rush and the seemingly impossible becomes possible.

My task was to pull delicate threads together and weave those threads into an exquisite tapestry. Sometimes I had very little information about one of the stories and would need to persist to get the necessary details. At times, my questions would surprise Joseph, for the extraordinary is so much a part of his ordinary. My one desire was that I would become so transparent that what would be given in this text would be "pure Joseph." I wanted others to experience what I had in working on this book, a sense of falling in love with life and being induced into a higher level of consciousness.

It has been said, "Without a vision, a people perish." Within the last decade there has been a reemergence of myths, a retelling of the great stories. Myths hold the power to rekindle vision, for they speak the language of the soul. Through the work of Joseph Campbell, Jean Houston, Robert Bly, Jean Bolen and countless others, we have been awakened to the possibilities of the heroic journey, the quest, and the rites of passage, tasks, and initiations along the way. Myths give us the map to that journey, showing us how to separate from the familiar, how to resolve differences and meet challenges, and then to return as a more integrated self. Myths inextricably link us to the mystery of the cosmos and to the natural world around us. Ultimately, they connect us more deeply to ourselves.

The gift of Joseph Rael is to help us cross the threshold from the place where we tell the myth and move to the place where we become the myth.

Joseph speaks from the place of the myth-maker. His vision, personal stories, and teaching re-enchant life. They come from a place of innocence and purity, from the transcendent realm, where a thin veil separates the seen from the unseen world. As we hear his stories, our chords of memory are stirred and we are inspired to the Greater Self. We, too, slip into those places "where God hides," where all becomes the silence, and then listen within while that Presence speaks.

The call that Joseph presents is not to try and

emulate his life but to enter our own lives more coura-
geously, more passionately, more genuinely. We are inspired to trust the truth of our own visions and of our own
discoveries and to dare to live that truth. The challenge,
then, is to be the creative myth-maker that we are, to
consciously choose our myth, lest it be chosen for us by the
collective mind. We are empowered to live the symbolic
life, to experience all life as the metaphor of the mind of
God.

MARY ELIZABETH MARLOW
Virginia Beach, 1993

Life is the road of Goodness.

Life is connected to time

as crystallized meanings.

Life purifies itself with heart connection

so it can ascend beyond the heavens as
radiating innocence.

CHAPTER ONE

BORN INTO VIBRATION

Bonding with the Land

When one grows up in the ancient teaching that everything is metaphor and is a resonating energy of the Great Spirit, then all life is sacred.

The Picuris pueblo where I grew up was a living being with a psyche of individuals made up into a group that I began to know as my father's people. The village was architecturally designed so it would continually give sustenance to the people who lived there. Because we were there we lived our moments inside resonance. The village was not just a physical place, it was a mental, an emotional, and a spiritual place as well.

The design of the architecture was made from ancestral memory and of moments not yet born and the opportunity to explore potential. There was purpose in both the design of the houses and the layout of the village. The women were the descending light principle, therefore they were in charge of the household. And yet the houses were square, the shape symbolic of the masculine. The men, on the other hand, went into kivas for their spiritual training, and the kivas were round, the shape symbolic of the feminine. Even as a boy of six or seven, already the round structure of my femininity was expanding the potential in my masculinity because alchemically I was growing into my opposite, that I might learn balance of male and female. What was being taught was that one first accepts the energy that he/she is born into and then learns its opposite, so that one can become integrated and balanced.

As children we were taught that we existed as pressure point activators for the sacred sites within the village. Every twenty feet or so were consecrated points on the ground which carried special blessings. These shrines were buried in the ground and were only visible to the inner eye.

As we walked through the village, we pushed them into aliveness with our bodies' pressure on them. Because we lived as energy, we began to understand that everything in each designated location was the resonating vibration of the play of principal ideas. The holy shrines were placed there because the vibrational essence of those holy sites would enhance the psyche of community and of each individual within community. The vibration would bond us to a love relationship, a knowing that life was in love with us, that we held the living life within our lives. This knowing kept me loyal to my beloved landscape.

A trail connected the lower village to the higher village, like the connection between the lower, middle, and upper worlds. Since all life is a metaphor, what was really happening when I walked twenty feet or so on the trail, was that I was connecting one vibration with another, one principle idea with another. In walking I was "Time and Purity, Beauty and Awareness of God's light." The village was architecturally designed so that the physical people lived alongside the supernatural beings who would manifest themselves through the sacred ceremonies. And the sites continually gave sustenance to the people who lived there. Superimposed on the physical village was the psyche of community and superimposed on the psyche were still many other realities, disappearing into infinity.

Living and walking in the village each day was like walking into myself, as a loving plane of existence. I used to jog, run, or walk through the village every morning just so I could get my loving pats from the village sites. There were the weathered pathways which wound their way among the adobe style structures, the open space in the center of the village, and the mountains in the distance. On early morning walks I used to enjoy breathing the familiar air. The fresh air, like a resonating intelligence hanging as a cover on the surfaces of the village, was delightful to drink into my lungs. Yet, each day the experiences were interestingly different and spatially new. It was not uncommon for me to walk into alternate realities unexpectedly. I would gaze at the light reflected on the golden micaceous clay of the adobe structures, or notice the play of the wind during the different hours of the day. I would pretend to disappear into the shadows and ride the giant trees, or be aware of what people and what situations would present themselves each day and quietly listen to what all of that was telling us. The energy was always shifting, was always different. The resonating vibrations in the sacred sites were always changing so that the people in the village were always alive with energy. These sacred spaces, generating life sustaining powers, maintained our integrity as a group, orienting each individual toward the community's highest ideals.

We knew we were a people (a "vibration") who had come from the Infinite Void, from zero, from one's sense that we did not exist. We were made of appearing and disappearing light that came from the inhalation and exhalation of God's breath. We were from the very Heart of the center of the non-existence of infinity.

Life in the village was centered on our being in harmony with our spiritual names. These spiritual identities were enhanced in three ways: through the use of breath in articulating our spoken names, through the materialization of our inborn gifts in the arts and music, and in the movements of our ceremonial dances.

Breath means life, so when a child was born and it was time for the naming ceremony, it was always done with breath. Breath is the way in which something material is created from the no-form place through movement. This would ensure that the child's identity, as its breathing, would stay fused as one with whatever it would bring into material form, while moving like a Tiwa-speaking being, made of sound. The Picuris child would always stay in touch with its tribal life because it belonged to three different levels — breath, matter, and movement. But the breath was what kept the other two levels connected as one.

Creativity was honored through the various forms of arts and crafts: pottery, weaving, drawing, painting, etc. These were all the ways for us to stay vital. We kept our identity through movement: purposefully walking, dancing, and by making ceremonies of daily life.

During certain periods of the year, there were plant dances and animal dances. Also there were songs and ceremonies for the sun and the moon. The various ceremonies were re-enactments of principal ideas. The water ceremony could have multiple meanings. For example, it might be a healing-heart ceremony for me at times, while at other times it was the way by which the loving vibration of time bonded with the lifting qualities of life. And this would happen because time was crystallized meaning that had the quality of liftingness. These two resonating vibrations of energy seemed to bond our personal vibrations to those of the village's resonance.

Whether it was through the ceremonies or through the sacred geometry of the architecture, or through the vibrational essence of the sacred sites, there was always the sense that the village was a cluster of souls that had come to live together in Picuris Pueblo. We had chosen to live as relatives, together, in community. There was the sense that together we could become part of the vibrations and emanations of the beauty of innocence. There is a lifting quality in community that brings forth an enhanced awareness through timeless living as one.

The Blue Stone People

In 1987 something very special happened to me. I had a visionary experience in which the veil that separates the third and fourth dimensional world was lifted. It was as though I was standing behind a curtain which was clear but not transparent. Suddenly, the veil was pierced and a hole began to grow larger and larger until there was an opening into another dimension. There before me appeared a vast horizon.

In the vision I saw Picuris Pueblo, New Mexico, as it was thousands of years ago. It was at a time when the ocean water, which had previously covered it, was gone. All that remained was a mud flat.

I saw two beings descending. They were sitting side by side, riding on some kind of transparent space machine, the dimensions of which could be sensed rather than seen. They came closer and closer towards a place near where my grandmother's house was later to be built. Eventually, they landed.

As soon as they landed, I knew who they were — two Kachina figures who had come to bring the spirit of life to the village. They were giant figures, at least ten feet tall, androgynous in nature, wearing long flowing black robes which contrasted sharply with the whitewash painted on their square-like faces. They landed at a place I could see had been previously designated as the sacred site for the new inhabitants who were to become the people high up in the mountains of north central New Mexico.

And then, without warning, they were transformed into He-She Blue-Stone people. In another moment, I saw overlays of rapidly changing landscapes until suddenly my grandmother's house appeared, as if coming out of the dawn-time of an early morning light and fresh air. There is a blue stone that sits outside my grandmother's house today. It is the same blue stone into which the Kachinas were transformed. At the time of that transformation, the stone was anchored into the earth and there it remains, a major power point whose effect has been experienced for generations and will be experienced for generations to come.

The vision then changed rapidly. I was moved through a time continuum. A dozen or so scenes flashed before me. I saw the formation of the rivers and the mountains, the heating and cooling of the earth, lush, green vegetation and brown, arid dryness. Each era, each landscape, was a new page flashed before my eyes and then blown away by vigorous wind. As each page was removed, another appeared. The scenes lasted for only seconds but contained an eternity. Finally, the shifts ceased, and one scene remained. The scene looked like Picuris as it was in 1940 when I first saw it with my child's eyes.

It wasn't until forty-seven years later, when I was in Pennsylvania, far from the Picuris area of New Mexico, that I had this vision and saw just where the blue stone had come from and what significance it had in my life. After I had my vision, childhood memories suddenly took on new meanings. As a child, I would watch and wonder as the people came to feed the blue stone. The people referred to the stone as the Blue-Stone people. They would honor the sacred site with gifts of corn meal. When I was a child, I used to see strange beings from other solar systems feeding the blue stone too. Perhaps it was a holy place for them as it was for us.

Our elders used to tell us that all holy sites are endowed with ancient wisdom. These centers have innate powers. Those who are sensitive and who spend time at these places absorb the power or pick up the information held there when their time comes to carry it. I think now that holy places often lie dormant for long periods because that which created the place waits and watches for a time when certain historic moments occur and conditions are set in place, conditions which allow wisdom to come through certain people who will bring it forth into the consciousness of that era.

Sometimes, the power waits for a child to be born who will live in or around that sacred site so the wisdom can be embedded in the tissue of the child's psyche. Individuals who are destined for that purpose will relate, explain, and translate what must take place next in the development of higher consciousness.

There is energy that comes to all of us from the sacred place, the vibrations of an ancient past, wisdom we would come to find one day. Once the sacred place is discovered, we begin to open to the wisdom. It descends upon us just as it did when the beings from the spirit of life brought spirit to the people.

House of Sound

I lived with my grandmother near the blue stone for about a year. I was fortunate as a young child to be able to spend so much time with her. According to my tradition, when a woman enters the period of her life between the ages of thirty and seventy, she carries the energy of descending light, of gifts being brought forth from the Heavenly Planes. In my grandmother's presence however, all I was able to feel was the energy of her love. Through her, light descended as warmth on us children.

My grandmother was small, probably no more than five feet tall. When I was a child, that felt reassuring, for it meant she was never far from my reach. Since she was pleasantly plump, hugs from her were especially warm and comforting. I never tired of gazing in her face. Her eyes were dark and shiny and when she looked at me, it was with such goodness that I knew she could see all the way into my heart. What I remember most was her smile. She seemed always to be smiling. Her whole face would light up from somewhere deep inside. For her, life was full of joy, and she had the capacity to tap into a pleasure, even while doing the simplest of tasks.

My grandmother's house was a simple, two-room structure with two windows and a door. The outer walls were slightly rounded and made from adobe, a mixture of mud, straw, and micaceous clay. When the sun shone, the tiny pinpoints of gold, which were everywhere in the micaceous clay, would reflect its rays, giving the whole house a glistening golden quality.

Inside, the walls were painted with red clay from the ground upwards for about three feet and were white-washed the rest of the way up to the ceiling. Overhead, the ceiling was constructed from pine poles which had been stripped of their bark.

Much of my grandmother's day was spent in the kitchen. The kitchen did not have a stove, so all of the cooking was done on an open fireplace in clay pots. I would watch with delight as she stooped over the fireplace. Her small, round body was just the right size to make the fireplace disappear! The light of the flames would some-how outline her moving silhouette on the wall. It seemed like magic to me.

After cooking, she would set about the other chores. She would sweep the floor with a hand-brush of straws harvested from the fields. These brushes were holy because the herb the straw was taken from was sacred. Thus, sweeping the floor and cleaning the house was really a ceremony of beautification, opening the gateways to the upper heavens, to awareness. She managed our lives with tasks geared toward work as worship, as ceremony in our daily lives. As she swept the earthen floor, she would create a small dust-storm in which she would periodically disappear. Then, out from the dust, we would see the familiar, small, plump figure emerge once more. When she was sweeping, we would all try to keep out of her way because, in her path, we knew nothing was safe. Dust, she would say, was the principle of transcendence.

She would shout to us, "Pay attention!" so that we wouldn't miss the voices of our ancestors who were there to help us to be good people. If we missed their voices, we could get lost in the metaphors of life. So we would be swept playfully out of the door along with the flying dust and then she would shout, "Be sure to leave your shoes at the door before you come back in, you little dust beings!"

Just as soon as the dust settled, we would see our grandmother scurrying down to the river to quickly refresh herself before scurrying back up to the house to continue with the daily chores. She knew we only had such a short time in which to live and that we should therefore live as solidly as we could so we could appreciate every moment.

In my grandmother's house we did not have any

furniture. It was particularly significant that there was no table, so we would sit on the dirt floor when eating. "The floor is important," my grandmother would say. "It represents the floor of life where everything comes from. It holds everything. Everything that comes, comes from the floor, or the foundation of life. It feeds us, it clothes us, it houses us." She would make reference to the fact that our houses were made from adobe, from earth, and so we were being supported by the soil of the earth, which symbolized the vastness of the inner self. The earth was the flower garden and we were her little flowers.

So when we ate sitting on the floor, we were in prayer, being fed, and in turn, we were feeding the being that was feeding us. Our grandmother would feed us from clay dishes and we would eat with tiny gourds, which we used for spoons.

Once we were busy eating our soup with the special gourds, she would take the opportunity to tell us stories. "These gourds are made of music," she would tell us, "and so all the food you eat comes from beautiful music. You are eating music so your bodies will make beautiful, sacred sounds, sounds which will make your personal songs. The house that we live in is made of sound and life is a house made of sound and the people are made from that sound.

"Since people are made of sound, listening is important. It is through listening that you become a true human, and a true human is a listener who is constantly attuned by working with everything that is happening.

"To become a true human, one must become conscious of listening and hearing the voice of the Great Mystery speaking through everything, through the sound of a tree, or the bird flying overhead, or the wind in the room, or someone breathing, or someone talking, or a moment of silence. The activity of sound is what made the people. It is, therefore, simply through listening, and using that listening and paying attention, that one finds the guidance of the Great Mystery along the path of life."

She used to say that our house was modelled after the first house, created out of the shattering light of our ever-unfolding perceptions. As she spoke, we knew the whole universe was alive and everything had perception. All of the principal ideas which made the floor and the walls and the doors, or the fresh air, or the sunrises, the noontimes, the sunsets, were all moments in which everything was being perceived by the essence of the Great Mystery and the Great Mystery was being perceived in return. The "House of Shattering Light" was a dimension of this perceptual reality which was taking place moment by moment as we expressed ourselves mentally, emotionally, physically, or spiritually.

We live in the world of the "Shattering Light." We are simply a moment in eternity. We are but a ringing-bell slice of light and through that slice, we can see. We are in touch with that moment mentally, emotionally, physically, and spiritually. However, the ringing slice of light passes quickly and we are then involved in the next slice of light and the next moment. There again, we see it mentally, emotionally, physically, and spiritually. Soon this slice of light too is gone and we are into the next slice of light, and so it continues. One day, in a shamanic experience, I saw that we were created out of the continuum of rapidly moving light and I saw that it was timeless in its nature.

In the House of the Shattering Light, time has an opportunity to become, and meaning slows down, so we can perceive each moment and participate in it totally, for very soon that slice of light gives way to another. My grandmother taught us that living inside the perceptual reality would keep us in fine attunement because we would be totally aware of what was transpiring, moment by moment, in our lives.

When the stories and the teachings were over for the day, I would sometimes stay sitting on the floor enjoying the warmth of the fire. The air seemed full of magic; the flames would dance before our eyes, filling the whole room with a soft glow. It was like being in a warm and comforting womb. Time would disappear. Sometimes the light would cast mysterious shadows on the wall. A thousand stories would come from those forms, the images, often of animals, the familiar forms of the deer, the rabbit, the fox. This is not surprising when one considers that these animals were my playmates, my trusted friends.

It was in the world of nature that I felt most secure because it had the quality of love carrying me. By contrast, I felt so displaced at the school I attended. Here the days were intolerably long and time moved ever so slowly. I could not read until I was twelve. It took me that long to discover how to mentally bring the blackboard forward so that my poor eyesight was no longer a hindrance. Until that time I would escape whenever possible from anything connected with school or books and flee to the safety of the mountain range close to Picuris. Here I could learn from another teacher. Here was the wisdom of Father Sky and the nurturance of Mother Earth. Here my animal friends would share their secrets. I would stay for hours, for days at a time, alone and never lonely. I would run and play, free in the wildness and beauty of the world surrounding me. Here was pure being, where my body could drink the early morning crispness and the evening bird songs. It was here I fell more in love with life and grew in awe of the Spirit from which all comes. The carrying qualities of beauty began to drink me into their revelations.

Teachings from a Medicine Man

In my early years I heard stories about my grandfather on my father's side but did not know him very well because some of those early years were spent at the Ute Reservation of my mother's people in Colorado. However, when we moved to Picuris, home of my father's people, I was given my first opportunity to know a person who was not just my grandfather but also a wise man.

My father had told me that there would be a time when he would place me in the home of my grandfather. Not much more was said about that until the day came. I remember ceremoniously walking on my father's right side while momentarily hesitating on the holy sites so that I could "juice" up with their essences. Leading me down the dirt path was not easy for him, so he kept saying, "Come, come, pay attention," as we made our way through the village houses, until we arrived at the house of my grandfather. My grandfather's name was Antonio De Simbola; his Tiwa name was Pel Qui Weh.

"I have brought you this boy so you can teach him how the people descended then arose as the people," my father said. I knew this was an important rite of passage for me. My grandfather seemed pleased, and his wife, with her arms reaching out almost as far as her warm smile, came forward to welcome me. My father then left and I lived there for awhile. How long I lived there I don't remember. Time seemed like many winters and many summers of passing images — truth feeding life into my presence.

Living with my grandfather was living with the unpredictable. I never knew what he was going to do next. I would get up in the morning in hopes that he had not left the house. I always woke up on the run because I didn't want to miss anything. Wherever he walked and whatever he became involved in seemed to be infused with magic. I remember once I dislocated my knee. My grandfather was five miles away and "heard" me and came home immediately. He then proceeded to place ashes on my knee. It healed instantly! The vitality which resonated from his presence affected everything. It was as though he left tiny whirlwinds of energy in his path, energy for those who followed to pick up.

In later years, I remember riding a motorcycle with my brother. We would come up close behind these large semi-trucks so that we would be able to turn off our motor and let the convection carry us along the highway. Of course, it was dangerous; had the truck stopped we would have run into the back of it. But we thought it was fun. Like my grandfather, I loved the unpredictable; but, unlike my grandfather, I had much to learn about the difference between the creative edge and the dangerous edge.

My grandfather was a very well-rounded person and was held in high esteem by the community. Because he was a Medicine Man and could speak Spanish as well as Tiwa, he was invited in among the Hispanic people in our community as a spiritual teacher.

Much to my delight, my grandfather would take me with him and I would repeat the Hail Marys and Our Fathers at the Hispanic people's church. The only problem was that all of the prayers were done kneeling. I would stay kneeling for as long as I could and then my knees would begin to hurt. I would become fidgety and want to get up, but I knew that I couldn't because my grandfather wouldn't like it, so I suffered in silence. Soon I discovered a way of overcoming this discomfort. I decided that my knees simply weren't there and if they weren't there, then they couldn't feel the pain. (I would later learn that this is a technique of intercepting pain used in many circles.)

As I knelt next to my grandfather, trying to ignore the pain, I found that I could pass very quickly into places where I could see angelic beings created by the energy of prayer. I could never hear what it was they were saying, although their mouths were moving constantly, but it was fun to watch them flashing through walls. It was like enjoying my own movie, one that no one else could see. I wanted so much to share it with them but I could not because I knew they could not see it. Whenever I closed my eyes I was able to continue to watch this "movie" and, at the same time, hear, way in the distance, the murmuring prayers of the people. After a while I became disoriented. I was no longer able to hear my grandfather. All I was aware of was a brilliant light swirling around the room, a nurturing light, bluish-purple in color, which enveloped me as tenderly as when my father use to hold a lamb. The forms in the room and the people almost seemed second-ary to this vision. It was as if the physical world were an afterthought. The real form of life was in the light of the dancing vibration of prayer.

During the stay with my grandfather, I began to learn the Tiwa world, the world of the people, who, according to the teaching of my grandfathers and my grandmothers, came from sound, from vibration. According to the Tiwa myth-maker being, in the beginning Vibration wanted to walk, Vibration wanted to run, Vibration wanted to climb. According to the storyteller, Vibration loved to climb, like little boys love to climb. Vibration liked to sit and play, just as little boys like to sit and play. Vibration liked to be grandfathers and grandmothers. Vibration loved little boys and little girls because Vibration was babies and Vibration was boys of eight years old or girls of eight years old or teenage girls and boys. Vibration was made of teenage love already being what it was being, so it could continue. Vibration was twenty and then twenty-five and then thirty-five or thereabouts.

Then Vibration decided that it would descend into form and become the living concreteness that we call the material form. It was in repeating its form over millions and millions and millions of moments and light years that it was finally embodied, becoming what it had always loved to do the most and that was vibrating—vibrating as humans do and as energy does in the physical world or conceptual world, as the action states of various conscious awarenesses.

What this myth was telling us was that if we were to do something long enough and believe in it, we could manifest it. We were receivers of memory, listening stations of cosmic truths in the here and now, and senders to the future.

My grandfather would often take me with him to the kiva. In the summertime, we would even sleep there. One particular summer evening I shall never forget.

As usual, my grandfather built a fire in the fireplace but, this time, after he had finished singing a number of songs and prayer lines on the floor of the chamber, he asked me to lie down beside him and to put my back against his when we went to sleep. He said that there would be some dreamtime and there might be some lights and some other phenomena and for me not to be afraid because the human back is sacred.

He lay down with his body facing the fire. I can remember that he was blocking off most of the heat with his body. So, in order to keep warm, I kept snuggling my back close into his back. I know now why he had me lay on my side in that posture. My grandfather talked about the transmission of knowledge as one of the ancient practices. He told me that the front part of the body receives information and the back passes it on. That is why we have a front side and back side of the physical body. With the front we face situations, we face life, we walk into things, we meet people face on. The front side receives heat from psychic energy, and the back side is the cold "chi" side. We are like miniature translators and transformers. We are simply transmitting or broadcasting. We are little broadcasting stations that openly bridge the future while washing all our moments with memory. That is how come we know things.

This energy goes out through the backs of our bodies. These are the tracks that we leave behind, physically as well as philosophically. We leave behind certain works we create and we leave those works for people who are, therefore, followers. So when we say "people who follow us" it is a literal as well as a philosophical statement of the purpose of life itself. We are simply actors in this life unfolding before us and, as we face life, we leave behind our trail of moments for those who come behind us to resonate to.

When I lay down back-to-back with my grandfather, I saw brilliant flashes of light. Later I realized that those lights, which were coming on and off, off and on as I closed my eyes, and perhaps continuing after I went to sleep, were lights coming out of his body. They were the different powers in ideas that were presently living in all things of the village. They lived within us and in our relationships with other planets and stars. The lights also were the awakening, in and of themselves, the awarenesses which opened our eyes to life and the part we played in it. They held too, the sense of being in the state of grace, constantly falling back unto itself, that sense that comes to us in those moments when we feel that we are being carried. Above all, there was a powerful sense of wholeness or holiness in those lights because they were made of a sleeping dark night time that was planting lights on its dark fields.

As the transference took place, the knowledge was passed from his consciousness to mine. At the time of that experience with my grandfather, Tiwa wasn't written and is still not written today. I believe that experience translated the sound vibration of the Tiwa language. That vibration would create in me an awe of life. Due to that moment I would want to investigate the sounds of the different languages and would search for the Mother tongue. Out of that moment would come the longing and wanting that created the impetus to write this book based on sound vibration language.

Through that experience I came to understand that the earth has always been talking to us, but many of us have lost our sensitivities to sound and to vibration, so we do not hear her. Through sound she is telling us exactly what is going to happen next, but we haven't been able to hear her because we have lost our sensitivity to work as worship. We have forgotten how to listen to what our efforts have been saying.

One of the last teachings of my grandfather was "Pay attention!" I didn't understand what he meant. I know now he was saying that the key to life is sensitivity and that only through developing the capacity of sensitivity to everything will we hear the real message.

"*Ah dah la pi ah chi*" were the words my grandfather used, "Become the essence of work, the being of listening, if you want to be a true human being. Become of work, of listeningness, and you will find the voice of our Mother/Father spirit talking."

CHAPTER TWO

UNLOCKING
VIBRATION

Looking for the Infinite Self

 The focus of my whole life became to understand all physical forms as sound and vibration of the infinite Self and to be a working-listener to those forms. For me, listening, seeing, and working all were the same. As long as I could remember, I had investigated the infinite Self by listening to and watching the push-pull vibrations in physical motion. I had tried to understand the Self by becoming the relationship between those vibrations.

Even the ordinary events of life offered opportunities for learning to listen, for learning to see life in the movement of work as worship, and for learning the relationship of listening and work to the mysteries of vibration.

As a young boy I would sit down inconspicuously at meal time, eat my food, and talk with family members. From all outer appearances, everything seemed quite ordinary. My real attention, though, was seldom on the meal but was focused instead on discovering the significance of the forms that were present at the table, like the plate or the spoon or the cup. I wanted to understand the deeper mysteries. There was the sense that if I could tap the vibrational essence of these forms, therein might be the keys to understanding how the vibrational essences of all forms were working themselves alive. The energy of vibration is alive, and because it is alive it sees, it listens to the activity of work that is being created by its own vibration.

I began my journey into sound and vibration using the familiar, my native language Tiwa. To me, Tiwa is the language of nature, words made from the audible sounds that occur moment by moment in the natural environment in each twenty-four-hour day.

Take my name, for instance. As a concept in English, Beautiful Painted Arrow is simple enough. But when I say my name in Tiwa, *Sluu teh koh ay*, I hear an arrow arch through the air, strike something, quiver, and radiate energy in all directions. It paints beauty everywhere. That is the way with Tiwa. Everything that is said conveys a metaphoric sense of life, of time, of space. Everything is made up of principal ideas, and for each idea there is also a sound. So we are all made up of sounds, of listeningness, of seeingness, and of workingness. We are all music. With each inhalation we identify our purpose to be alive, vibrations of the here and now, and our universe is created. And with each exhalation, the universe is given new life. This is how we create the future; what we choose to live in each and every moment resonates outward on our breath. We inhale in one moment, and we are presentness; we exhale in the next, and we are futureness.

In 1946 I moved from my grandmother's house in Picuris to the house of Where Eagles Perch. In this house was furniture, and a wood stove. Sitting at the kitchen table, I would sound the word for plate or spoon in Tiwa. Then, I would let those sounds resonate throughout my body, my being. I would continue listening until the sounds went beyond audible sound into the vibration of my physical body in the silence of intuitive thought. From that sacred space, insights could come. I knew then that my main purpose in life would be to work-listen-see the self-empowering qualities of principal ideas, bringing them from their place of intuitive silence. I learned I could go into the place where they lay hiding and I could draw them out. I drew them into expressions as metaphors to stand alongside experience.

Soon, I proceeded to yet another level of discovery. I would listen to the sound that was made if you tap a cup or put a plate down on the table again and again. I would listen to the reverberations and let that sound carry me deeper into myself.

I became interested in following the sounds back to the origin of the forms of the plate or the cup or the spoon. I would ride on their sounds and go back to originality. Did these and other forms come from necessity because necessity is the mother of invention and when there is a need, something is invented to fill that need?

The very nature of vibration is such that I can follow

it back to its source and its creative emptiness which lies within it. In that creative silence it will automatically create a need, and then in the next moment, it invents something to fill that need. In this evolutionary process, vibration will tend to create its own inner meaning and, interestingly enough, materialize it. So nothing is really separated from itself but is inwardly and outwardly flowing, the continual manifestation of energy. Since the human being is also energy and since thoughts are also vibration, then everything is taking care of itself. That is the very nature of vibration on this plane.

A real breakthrough came when I made a transference from Tiwa to English. I discovered that the same insights that I was getting through Tiwa could also be discovered by using the vowels of the English language and sounding the vowels of each word. (The process of how to do this will be explained in Chapter Four).

When I added the study of Spanish, a third language, I began to slip through into other dimensions, making discoveries beyond just words and definitions of words. In fact, when anyone studies language, particularly when one studies more than one language, at some point there comes the knowledge that the language he is studying, whatever language that may be, is a language of power.

Throughout history we have developed socio-economic and political systems taking into account only the logical surface of the language that we use. This is the left-brained, rational approach to language. In finding solutions to a problem, we use logic to reach higher states of consciousness. For example, take a simple sentence, "I will call you." For all practical purposes, this statement has meaning purely on a ordinary logical level. But through studying the sound vibrations of the words, I am able to go deeper, to re-evaluate the meaning of language.

There are, in fact, two levels of meaning with every sentence, the logical level or orientation, and a second level of meaning, the creative level or orientation. At the creative level, "I will call you," translates into the vowel sounds "aah eee aah uu," and is saying "perfection of awareness" and the "innocence of carrying."

Components of Language

Language is essentially a series of physical sounds that we create while speaking to tune our bodies. We created language to keep reminding ourselves that our physical form is made up of three things: spirit, matter and movement. Spirit is synonymous with the breath of life. It is here that ideas are born because this is the purifier or the heart level of the Infinite Self. It is here that we have awareness, awareness of all things, of all parts of self, and therefore we are whole. The sound associated with Spirit is "eee," or awareness.

Breath, materialism, and movement together make up the cosmic mother/father idea. The feminine principle is the light which descends from them, from the cosmic mother/father. The sound associated with matter is "aah" of the washing, purifying breath, which permeates all of the physical realms of movement.

The masculine principle is movement, the movement within all things. The masculine is the extension of the feminine. This is the place of inner sight, as in the word "insight." The sound associated with movement is "oh."

"Oh" is innocence, selflessness constantly renewing self by allowing self to reach beyond. Innocence is one's true purpose. Here one finds truth without manipulation by anything or anyone.

Character of Life

Language was created to reflect the qualities of life. As I studied language, I began to uncover the deeper mysteries of the meaning of each vowel sound:

"Aah" (the A sound in Spanish) - *Purification*

"Eh" (the E sound in Spanish) - *Relationship*

"Eee" (the I sound in Spanish) - *Awareness*

"Oh" (the O sound in Spanish) - *Innocence, the Infinite Void*

"Uu" (the U sound in Spanish) - *Carrying*

Inherent in the vibration of the vowel sounds are the qualities around which our whole social, economic, and political systems are based.

Take the sound "aah," which means "purification." Perhaps the intent behind war is purification. Or "eee," which means "awareness." Our educational systems, grants, programs of higher learning are all geared to enhance awareness in a particular area of life. "Eh," "relationships," would include all organizations, clubs, societies, and groups which endeavor to provide opportunity for people to support and coexist with one another, like Alcoholics Anonymous or cancer support groups. The quality of "oh," "innocence," would be reflected in the arts: music, theatre, painting, to mention just a few. "Uu" means "carrying." For example, banks carry loans, transportation systems carry people, and social systems help carry burdens. We even speak of political candidates carrying a state.

For the most part, we are unconscious of the deeper mysteries inherent in the vowel sounds. By chanting (methods given in Chapter Four) we consciously invoke our connection with their qualities.

Mysteries of Metaphor

In my research with vibration, I was also learning that the forms of the plate or the cup or the spoon are profound metaphors. One of the aspects of the spoon's vibration means beauty, so when we use the spoon to eat, what we are doing is feeding beauty into ourselves. And the plate is the symbol of the slice of light that allows us to go beyond time into timeless awareness. When we eat out of the plate, we are eating the food that on an energetic level has been fused with the plate's energy of timeless awareness. Hence, we can say we are feeding beauty and timeless awareness into ourselves. The table on which the plate is sitting vibrates as the metaphor for the plane of goodness. The plane of goodness is where God's plan for us sits. Therefore, the act of sitting down at the table to eat is a profound spiritual ceremony in itself. Whether we sit down at a kitchen table or at a desk, we are being fed by our inner plane of goodness. We are manifesting some good effort out of what we do with our time.

When we sit at a table, sometimes we watch the clock, as though at some innate level we want to understand what time is. That is because, in reality, time and awareness are integral parts of movement. Once we understand what movement really means, we can then see our patterns of behavior. There is an ancient saying that a confused state is that state in which the idea has not yet begun to sing its song of identity.

Once the metaphor of the principle idea was understood through the mysteries of vibration, it fell in love with life and gained the curiosity to explore an infinite variety of forms. Similarly, my awe for life came out of this same tradition. I know that now.

What is a house? I have come to understand that a house is the form (or house) of the shattering light. The house is a metaphor to explain that there is a vibration in each moment, each moment is like a house, and a house is like a moment. In each moment that we live there is an opportunity to change ourselves in some way. We shatter what we were in the past, so that in the new moment we can remake ourselves. In a day's time, we go through many different moments, many different opportunities to remake ourselves and therefore evolve. To understand the metaphor of the house of shattering light is to know that we are continually in a state of evolution.

What is a road or a path? The road is the metaphor for the head of the family of ideas continually investigating themselves to find out who they are being in every single moment. Because we are changing constantly, we have to be continually investigating ourselves. Otherwise, we lose who we really are. Another meaning for road is the direction or form by which our fears are challenged and the manner in which we face them.

The door space on a house is the metaphor for the face, for only by facing life can we enter it. Similarly, a moment has a door through which we enter it. The outside of a house or the outside of the moment is where initiation lives, because it faces itself. The face is really the metaphor for entering. Therefore, initiation is the inside preparing the outside to manifest itself. The profile of vibration is made that way.

This is another way of saying that silent energy is called forth by audible sound and vice versa. The audible sound calls out the silent sound or vibration. It comes out with renewed strength and power and it re-grounds and re-enlightens audible sound so there is continuity. Vibration does not cease to exist but continues. So there is first the audible sound, as with the chanting of the vowels; then there is the silent sound, the place where Inspiration hides.

Silent Sound: Where God Hides

There are two aspects of vibration, audible sound and silent sound. To give an example using the computer: when the vibration is in the state of silence, the silent sound, it is like the computer searching for answers. It is looking for its form; it is searching for what it is going to manifest. The audible sound comes after silence has found its manifestation. It becomes a live sound. That live sound has an attribute or quality to it that is saying yes to life, saying yes to itself, to that impulse, yes to whatever it is that it wants to manifest. It is saying yes to the apple tree to be an apple tree or the plum tree to be a plum tree. The energy of life is flowing in that vibration through the loud (audible) sound of calling, which is tuning up that metaphor that it is wanting to substantiate, so that it can be in existence, be alive, and grow.

If you were to draw a tree and draw where the tree roots go into the ground, the part of the tree above ground would be the area of audible sounds and the root of the tree would be the area of the silent vibrations. In order to manifest itself, the silent vibration needs to come above the ground, and then it becomes audible sound. This tree is the cosmic brain. The ground, or the surface of the earth, is where we enter into the inner cosmic self.

Walking with intent and ceremonial dancing are ways to connect with the inner, infinite self. The metaphor that is enacted is the collision of the foot with the ground. The foot is how we move out in life. In ceremonial walking and dancing, the foot connects with the ground, which is the symbol of the infinite self.

The earth is such a powerful metaphor of truth that vision questors will dig a hole in the earth and go down into the hole in order to be more in tune with that silence fused with perfection. It is not surprising, then, that the chambers for teaching the ancient mysteries were underground. Going underground was the metaphor for entering the perfected self.

As a young boy, I was taught in those underground chambers to look within. I discovered I was silence and darkness. And then I saw that by seeing with my eyes I created movement and out of it illumination came, and then I realized the silence and the darkness were full of emptiness, and the emptiness was full of light.

Tiwa: The Mother Tongue

Since the basis of my training in sound is from Tiwa, it is important to understand what Tiwa is. Tiwa is an ancient tongue, but not an Indian language. Instead, it is a language that was constructed according to the different vibratory levels of mother nature. According to the ancients, language is an enormous ball of whirling energies which came from the being of goodness. Out of this whirling ball, the Creator created the different languages, each with specific differences, each made from resonating qualities of goodness. Every single form has its own specific vibration that is different from the next one.

The people who use Tiwa language today are the Picuris, Taos, and Sandia Pueblo Indians in New Mexico and the Isleta Pueblo Indians in Texas.

In recent years there has been a renewed interest in researching the origin of language. An article in the November 1990 *US News and World Report* entitled "Mother Tongue" focused on research by linguists as they work back from modern speech to re-create the first language of the human race. The presence of similar sounding words with similar meanings in two different languages suggests that the languages had a common ancestor. For example, take the word "water." It is *haku* (Proto-world) *hakw* (Amerind) *kwa* (Dene-Caucasian) *haku* (Nostratic) *hakw* (Indo-Europena) *aqua* (Latin) *wazzar* (Old German) and *water* (English). Sir William Jones, a Sanskrit scholar, discovered amazing similarities between Sanskrit and Latin and Greek, all root languages, indicating that Latin, along with Greek and Sanskrit, had descended from an even more ancient mother tongue.

Did Tiwa come before Sanskrit or did Sanskrit precede Tiwa? Did Latin precede Tiwa or did Tiwa precede Latin? And what about Greek? What came first? According to Tiwa thought, first there were "the people" and "the people" means vibration. Did "the people" (vibration) create Sanskrit, Latin, Greek, and Tiwa? In Tiwa thought, the answer "yes" is what created the blood of life. "The people" were vibration, constructed by four processes: descending, arising, purifying, and relativity.

Language is the tuner sound, the sound that fuses descending and arising light in the crystallized meaning of time. And beyond language and sound is silence. Did silence create all of the different languages because it knew that the different languages would be a pathway to materialization of concepts? Perhaps we were made by God when He found He could make concreteness through sound. He made vibration, He made form, and as He played with various forms and vibrations in that time which was before time, we were created in the image of Cosmic Mother/Fatherness.

Purpose of Oral Tradition

The Tiwa people did not want to stray even one tiny increment from truth. They decided to keep Tiwa in the oral tradition because the oral sounds, like mantras of eastern religions, awaken inner mental knowing. Also, they knew writing makes language subject to interpretation, and once one begins to interpret language, it begins to write its own truth and we lose real truthfulness. A spoken word sound has meaning beyond itself and makes images. Language is made of completed forms as well as forms not yet finished or completed.

The nations who chose to write language down

chose to do so because they were interested in understanding power. They were interested in controlling memory. Writing language down meant that energy would crystallize and become reflective. It would stop the free flow of the vibrating essence that is continually re-nourishing our memories. In other words, writing language down allowed loss of recall. The vibrating essence of spoken language provides a way to keep a pure, verbatim mind through the practice of speaking. The vibration of the breath in speaking gives us a direct sensory connection with memory, so that past memory, the future, and the present stay together as one resonance.

Writing originated in vibration, because the very nature of vibration is made of three parts: past, present and future. The memory of the past comes with us as energy in our present moments and it is the energy that helps us to enjoy our goodness while the aspect of vibration having to do with futureness gives us clairvoyance. The aspect of vibration that is presentness grounds both past and future, and it places us.

The ancient ones were interested in mental telepathy, direct communication with Spirit. They knew everything is alive, everything is simply an opening to connect with the Omnipresence. They said we are going to dialogue with vibration because we know where the power is. Native American thought is about the power one can have that is the basis for miracles. I am not talking about the power to control someone or something, I am talking about the power of allowing the Omnipresence to work through you and to help you achieve higher consciousness, which is the purpose of our being here. We are Spirit. We just happen to be sitting around here in these bodies which we inherited from our mothers and our fathers. We borrow these bodies, we come here, and we experience life.

Becoming a True Human

In the language of nature, working and listening are the same. Working, or listening, means sensitivity. To be sensitive is to be aware, to listen with the body, which is really our ears, and to perceive what is going on around us with our listening mechanisms rather than our seeing mechanisms. This is because our seeing mechanisms can be illusionary. If we see without including that inner sensitivity, we do not get the clear picture of what is occurring.

During a recent trip to Germany, I was preparing for a sweat lodge ceremony, so offered a prayer with tobacco, sacred symbol for the heart. I put out the cigarette and placed the butt in my coat pocket. I intended to go to the house, leave my coat and other belongings there and head to the sweat lodge. Suddenly, two birds flew very close above my head. I knew something was up because birds just don't fly that close to anybody. The noise they made seemed to say, "Don't go in yet!" and so I listened.

Instead of going to the sweat lodge, I walked slowly while listening with the skin cover of my whole body as I walked into a nearby greenhouse. After I was inside a short time, I started to smell smoke. I was thinking, "Who in their right mind would smoke in a greenhouse? It is not healthy for the plants!" Then, I realized the smoke was coming from my coat pocket. The cigarette butt was still alight! Had I not been aware of the cue from the birds, I would have gone to the house, taken off my coat, and gone into the sweat lodge for several hours. In that length of time, the house might have burned.

A True Human Is a Listener

The true human is someone who is aware, someone who is, moment by moment, totally and completely merged with life. He is a listener. She is a listener. Out of that capacity of inner and outer listening, comes the quality of humility. The true listener is no longer defined by desires or attachments. Instead, he or she is sensitized to consciousness.

Listening is understanding the mystery of vibration because listening has to do with the inner vibration of the descending intelligence of the moment. Meditators become silence so that they can go to true vibration, which becomes the audible workings of vibration, of which ideas are made.

Inner listeners, or people who are continually listening to life as it is unfolding, are true humans because they are picking up vibrational messages before the messages become crystallized energy or perceptual forms that can then be articulated by the brain. Sensitivity, then, is paramount in developing the ability to be a good listener. In that process of listening, the voice of guidance is found.

This is the place where inspiration hides. At this level of vibration, one receives direct knowing. Decisions which are made are right decisions for that moment because the energy that is being tapped is the voice of the intuitive silent vibration. I have found that any physical task, no matter how mundane, that allows me to apply effort, keeps me intimately connected to the source of creative insight.

A true human is a person who knows who he is because he listens to that inner listening-working voice of effort. Once he knows that, he knows the direction that he is to go because the inner voice will tell him exactly what it is he needs to do. One of the first things the true human learns is to look at life through the whole physical body.

Plowing is a metaphor for this physical way of looking at life. When we are plowing a field made up of consciousness, we are preparing the ground to plant a seed. So what are we plowing the field for? The farmer plows the field so that he can plant the seeds of a particular type that he wants to cultivate. What ideas do we want to cultivate? We study something and then walk it out so that we can plow the fertile field of consciousness and then move forth and plant the seed in that field that we have plowed, which in this case is our bodies. In that way, we plant what we cultivate in the weeks to come and eventually it produces its fruit.

The metaphor of playing is quite different. Playing means strengthening oneself. When we are playing, we are, in metaphor, making the self what it is becoming. Play time is an important aspect of building one's strengths, abilities, potentials, and capacities. Whether we are playing a violin or a guitar, or playing football, tennis, or cards, we are, through playing, making ourselves greater heart people.

In the act of living, we are emphasizing certain principal ideas about how life is. The true human is sensitive to what the metaphor of life really is, sensitive to play as a strengthening of the self, sensitive to walking as planting seeds of thought. This sensitivity is vital to us. Until we know what we are really being and what we are really doing, we may be unconscious of the energies we are producing, and these energies may or may not be ones we want to produce.

Listening Is Giving

For the true human, the first thing is to find out how to listen. Listening is different from seeing. Seeing, and the eyes, were created so we could move into things and through things. The ear, on the other hand, was created for the art of giving. One of the attributes of the ear is the give-away; to give into the effort of giving, to give into effort itself, the effort we can find in the toil of work in our lives. When we are listening, we are giving. When we are giving of ourselves, we are strengthening the work-listening-seeing aspect in ourselves. We are listeners to people's cosmic needs. First, we listen to what needs to be done, then we use our eyes to see what needs to be done. But if we start with trying to see what needs to be done we will miss the point and we will not really touch the basic humanity of the situation that is talking to us at that moment in time. So it is important to be sensitive to what qualities the ear brings and what qualities effort brings. Effort in the toil of our daily work is the food the planet earth eats for its survival.

Listening Is Working Action

Listening is working action. Action and vibration are the same, and action can be equated with struggle, or dynamic tension, the energy that is creating the possibility for creativity and then becomes the potential around possibility. Without that dynamic tension, there is no creativity. Out of that struggle of the creative energies, which is sound vibration, comes the reconciliation of that struggle and the manifestation of the creation of a new thing.

Wherever there is motion, the action of sight is there and there is the capacity of listening. Listening is action, listening is work, listening is vibration. So the people — which means "vibration" — came into being because their job was to create. When a nation, a society, or individuals no longer create, they begin to die because they are no longer part of action or movement. They are no longer the beings of listening, no longer the beings of giving to receive; therefore they are not receiving; they are not effort giving to effort. As a result, they cease to exist on the physical plane.

We become human in order to continue listening so that we can continue to verify that we exist. Without activity and action we cease to be. We no longer are alive. We are dead because we no longer belong in the realm of listening, or the realm of motion or activity. We die so that we can become memory, to give life to those who will continue to be astute listeners.

Once the being of listening is created it takes its place among all forms and they take places and become what they become — a tree becomes what it becomes, water becomes what it becomes, fire, air so on. Then all these elements begin to listen to each other because they are made out of greatness. And as they begin to listen to each other, they create the metaphors of different levels of consciousness that continually perpetuate life. And where are these reminders, if not in nature? All nature does is to continually remind itself who it is. Everything in nature, all of the landscape, trees, rivers, rocks, earth, and mountains are repeating who they are over and over again. That is how creativity and listening are kept alive, and that is the true nature of language. We are nature's music singing to God.

Listening Is Sensitivity to All Forms

In the film, *Dances with Wolves*, Lieutenant Dunbar is paid a high tribute when he is told he is becoming "a true human," meaning someone who is very sensitive. That would imply being sensitive to nature's resonance mentally, emotionally, physically, and spiritually.

If we want to be true humans, we become instruments sensitive enough for the forms to hone us, to sharpen and strengthen our mental, emotional, physical, and spiritual capacities for worship. If I talk about "treeness," for example, I become the pine tree and I let the tree speak through me. Even though I know what the pine tree is and even though I have already decided what the words are going to be, I let the energy of the tree speak through me nevertheless, because the tree, or whatever other form, can speak for itself better than I can. I am allowing that principal idea to speak through me, or me to speak through it, even though I am using words. And the pine tree said to me, "I am the Beauty of Carrying Light which is Washing Beautifulness with Colors of Joy," and then I became its form.

So in Germany, I could listen to the birds and they could tell me not to go in the sweat lodge, and Lieutenant Dunbar in *Dances with Wolves* listens to the wolf and develops a rapport with the wolf. If we develop sensitivity with one form, there is the likelihood we can be sensitive to all forms. We would know, as well, why a friend is hurting, because we would listen, even if there are no words. We become people who live our greatest potential in every single moment, wherever we are placed.

Before I learned that work is listening and worship, I used to sluff work as much as I could. I always chose to do things in the way that took the least effort. I thought the best way to live was to avoid work because it was not fun. Later I learned that the more effort I put into work, the better I felt spiritually, mentally, emotionally, and physically. As I worked harder, I felt more energetic. Working creates a vibration and changes us. Through work we increase our capacity to receive knowledge and impact the future.

When I became a good listener, it made me the greatest "giver" of life; it allowed me to serve in the highest way. I became a station that was receiving something and sending it right out. When I came from that place, I didn't have an argument with this religion or that religion, this ideology or that ideology. I became an instrument, simply a receiving station of the infinite void in that moment. I became a receiving station because I was completely present in the moment, a moment that was a living form that existed only to the degree of my highest effort.

These are the ancient mysteries. They were set up this way. In the end, the mystery is the infinite void and the mystery of the void is all of us remembering, because, truly speaking, we do not exist.

CHAPTER THREE

The MEDICINE WHEEL AS VIBRATION

Experiencing the Metaphor

Walking/talking is life breathing and materializing itself into the motion of the moment so that it can become real.

In the flash of light are the ashes that fly us beyond us in wisdom and into memory, placing us into the here of vigilance and the now of seeking. In the beginning was a flash of light in which everything was known and seen. In that moment was the beginning, the end and everything in between. The original vision came from this being we will call Inspiration, and we were that original vision. We are the original vision of the Being of Drinking Light, the soul.

That flash of light was a circle with a center made of heart and a periphery made of beyond. We, the Picuris, are at the center of the circle of light. We are the center to the north, to the south, to the east and to the west, to the up above and to the down below. We exist and we do not exist. We are the infinite void; we are relativity; we are awareness; we are "the people" which nature called, and "the people" which means vibration.

That flash of light is the "seed of life." Christians use the term "circle" of life, and others refer to it as the medicine wheel. These are all different terms for honoring, for celebration of the emotional, mental, physical, or spiritual essence of living breath.

Chief Seattle said that we are all connected because the circle of life is the light-seed of all life. The seed is in the land which gives us the initial clarity to discern right living. The land is the materialized vibration which forms our vibrations, as we live on it, work it, and eat the foods which grow from it. What's going on is that the heart is integrating with innocence, with teachableness, with that state in which there is no ego, when one is simply soaking it all up, like a sponge.

For anyone who has had a visionary experience, it is perhaps easier to understand how we became the original medicine wheel. When I had my first visionary experience, I got a flash of light, similar to the original flash of light that made us all, and then came the vision. In that instant, or in that flash of light, I saw days and years of experience manifested in metaphor as a vision. In a later visionary experience, I saw that light of whatever color was drinking itself into a vision of peace chambers or sound chambers. In this one flash of light, I saw how the chambers were to be built. It was like receiving four years of college in a single moment of time.

The mind can be seen as a circle. There are corridors from the center that lead out to the four directions, the East (the mental), West (the physical), the North (the spiritual), and the South (the emotional). When awareness expands, we move toward the outer periphery of the circle through one of these corridors while at the same time traveling from the periphery to the center. We begin to perceive certain forms and are given an increasing ability to dialogue with archetypes and principal ideas. As we evolve in consciousness, we go through different steps and therefore we perceive certain levels before graduating to other levels. Veils begin to disappear and we are able to know life more deeply. When those new levels are understood, we are given other levels; and when we are ready, we can perceive still higher levels.

Once, in a visionary experience, I had the opportunity to meet the "Lord of the Wind" riding in a chariot like Elijah in the Bible. My ability to have this experience, to meet this being, came only after years of studying the mysteries, of experiencing progressively greater capacities and levels.

As we reach the outer periphery of the circle, paradoxically we are, in that moment, in the middle of the circle. There is a greater knowing of the mystery behind the mysteries. This is not the knowledge of facts that comes as a result of reading hundreds of books or from studying a particular subject. Rather it is insight. This insight into the mystery of life came to me after I had been fasting and dancing for extended periods of time. That is how I understand it from my own experience, both from what I have learned in everyday life and from what I have experienced in the ancient ceremonies. It is through the hardship involved in effort as working-worship that I learned what vibration is all about. In my visions I received ceremonies which I have practiced in order to achieve certain mystical, spiritual initiations, graduating from one level to the next. I found that the way to access the wisdom contained in vibration was through the effort involved in the movement of dancing without food or water.

We have the medicine wheel because it is one way we can explain things to the rational mind. Where the circle ends and what is beyond the circle is not yet entirely known. What is known, though, is that the gifts lie outside the circle, and that they can be received through effort.

What is inside the medicine wheel is known. The heart is at the center of the Circle and there are the four directions, the east, west, south, and north. And though there are four directions, there is really only one direction, the direction of greatness, or the highest potential of goodness. It is the direction by which energy is continu-ously rediscovering itself. It draws from silence the sweetness of the milk of life. That is what it feeds on and that is what gives it life.

A mother knows she must feed her young baby and she gives her baby milk. Vibration is fed in a similar way. The infinite mother of the infinite self, which is the sky and the earth, feeds this child and then this child knows who it is and what it is to do and become. Since this child is continually in a state of becoming, it is continually descending as well as ascending while eating and drinking its sustenance from the mother of silence. We are aspects of the child of the lifting silence, of purity, and at times of the observer, observing the one observed.

So you see, the medicine wheel or circle really doesn't exist. It really doesn't exist because we don't exist. This has to be made very clear. We don't exist the way we think we do. We are energy that appears and disappears and appears and disappears. When it no longer is there, it automatically goes into silence. When it reappears again, it is not the same person because in some ways it has changed. And that is the key to evolution. Everything has evolved from something else to what it is now. That is how the future is part of the nature of vibration.

How the Medicine Wheel Works

Imagine the medicine wheel as a big circle, and in the middle of the circle is a stone which represents the heart. The inner periphery of that circle is made up of the unclarities that at this moment in time are there. The way the medicine wheel — or the circle of light — works is that in each given moment there is a flash from the center of the heart. It wants to know something that it doesn't know yet. This flash of light goes from the center to the inner walls of the circle. And in that moment of contact, it pushes the limits of wisdom outward and then swallows the new wisdom and returns it back into the heart center.

The center of the medicine wheel is the top of the mountain, and the mountain top is another metaphor for the heart. Vision questers go to the top of the mountain because walking the top of the mountain is synonymous with walking in the center of the cosmic medicine wheel. When a vision questor sits in the center of his circle on the mountain top and sends out thought, that which comes back to him from the periphery of that circle is the energizing vibration that keeps the vibration of life. In other words. the very nature of life is such that when the unclarities of the self which have been sent out in thought or deed return eventually back to the center of the circle of life, they enliven the existence of life at the center of the circle of light.

When the center of the medicine wheel sends an impulse, or a flash of light out to the periphery, it does so because it wants to know what it needs to be doing. That flash continues to go out and spread until it can no longer go and then it pulls from that dark void back to itself the survival power that it needs to go on to the next moment. All wisdom is stored at the periphery and beyond it. The unclarities that are in existence in the inner periphery are the ones that echo back meaning to the center of the Circle. That meaning is what gives life to the next moment, since each moment is a flash of light.

It is important to understand that an attribute of this light that comes from the heart of the medicine wheel is abundance. If abundance calls abundance, there is going to be more abundance. So when this flash goes out, it brings everything from all around the circle back to itself. Because it sends out abundance, it gets back abundance.

Another way of saying it would be to imagine a black empty space. In the middle of that darkness there is this flash of light like a tiny star that becomes larger and larger as it begins to light up a space which only moments before was blackness. As it lights up the darkness, this light, which is the light of the heart, realizes that it is really wisdom that is coming into conscious thought. But it doesn't realize it until the light goes out as far as it can and then hits the banks, similar to when you drop a pebble in the water and concentric rings form, moving outward toward the shore. These rings that go out are like this light that goes out. Finally, it reaches the bank. It can't go any farther because it has run out of steam. In coming back, it carries life sustaining energy because when this flash of light originates, it is asking for one thing, abundance of life. That abundance is made up not only of an idea or combination of ideas for that moment, for that heart center, but also, the abundance includes the power to carry through those ideas. That is how the circle of light functions. The circle of light has been with us, is always with us in each moment.

The other thing to understand about the circle of

light is that it is made up proportionally of two forms. One form is fear that it might cease to exist. In the Tiwa language, the word fear (*pi hu*) and the word heart (*pi neh*) have the same root. When fear enters, at this moment we have already begun to enter an altered state. Our hearts beat faster (making a sound like "*pi-hu-pi-hu-pi-hu*") and blood flows rapidly to the brain, sharpening our awareness. We are keenly aware of the one thin strand which separates life and death. In the moment of greatest fear we are closest to the moment of creation. This is because the other form of the circle of light is a need for awareness, for greater consciousness. Light is always chasing darkness, and darkness light.

Whatever the heart sends out, it receives back. We humans have that same pattern because we are made of vibration and patterned after the vibration of life. It is in our nature to send out things through thoughts and ideas because it is in our nature to behave like the rest of creation. However, we were given a mind to think in ways so that we can enhance life. We can consciously choose thoughts that are life-enhancing. But even if we have a thought that is not necessarily enhancing life, and we think that we have done something wrong, even that wrong move brings us back some good, maybe not in the immediate future but in its own time. In some way it is building the nature of life in us. Even something we might consider bad is good because it returns back to its origin a resonating vibration that sustains the heart of consciousness. It sustains the one single eternal flame of life whose sole purpose is keeping meaning alive so that life can continue having its purpose. Having purpose means having transformational potential, which is life's natural direction.

The heart of the medicine wheel is like a person, in metaphor, who stands at the top of the hill shouting out into a canyon. When this shout hits the canyon walls, it brings back with it its own echo. In that echo is contained the energizing force that revitalizes the center because of what it has to give. It is in that giving moment that life is receiving. So though the person shouts and the shout is carried out to the walls of the canyon and then back again, it is not until it returns back that it has meaning to the person who has sent out the shout.

Now the interesting thing about this is that as the impulse leaves the walls of the canyon back to the circle, it has enough time, or it gives itself enough time, so that when it reaches the center of the circle, it has already become a realized form; that is, it knows what it is when it comes into the center of the heart. It has cognizance. There is a space of time between the heart and the periphery when it can reveal its own meaning to itself.

A mundane example of how the medicine wheel works is the concept of gossip . The real reason we gossip about other people or find fault with other people is because we are really trying to figure out where we are placed in the moment and with ourselves. Perhaps we have low self esteem in that moment so we might gossip in order to make ourselves feel better. When we gossip, we send out some form of energy, a thought or an allegation. Since higher consciousness knows that we are really trying to find our way back to some inner harmony, the very nature of life is that it will send something back that will jar us loose and put us back into balance. All that life is really interested in is perpetuating itself beyond eternal unfolding of vast emptiness. It is continually looking at what it needs and then doing whatever it needs to do, including sending back what it has sent out, because it wants to restore harmony.

To explain using a different metaphor: When a new idea calls our attention to its reality, what is going on is that energy wants to lift us. It has nothing to do with whether that energy is good or not. It starts to lift us from where we were to a higher place where we can become what we are going to become next. That is the very nature of one of the mysteries of vibration. When it begins to lift to a higher level, something dramatic can happen. Then, we must die into new ideas and new forms. Death eats the old form, and then we can awaken. When perfection gives birth, we are born. We are not really awake until death renews life. Our moments of death awaken moments of birth, and this can happen once a year, or five or six times a day.

What is interesting about this lifting energy is that when it happens to us, it also happens to other people who are also being lifted to the next level. If we are being lifted, others are being lifted as well without necessarily being conscious of the process. They will be lifted to a level for a different reason, since not all of us are working on the same level at the same time.

When we began to lift ourselves from where we were before to a higher place, something dramatic happens in our lives. When energy is lifted in us to a higher level, that is our heart calling new forms. Why? Because the calling vibration changes into the body of the form concept that emanates as a new idea. Forms are created by energy that is lifting itself from where it was to where it wants to be next by calling its next highest achievement.

So, through us, life becomes aware, because life wants to experience itself through us, through our awareness. Life experiences beauty through the way. The way means being inside the purity of lifting, beyond time awareness, so that what we see and work is the beauty around us. Life is the ever-flowing presence here of ancient thoughts. Life wants to hang out with us and play and enjoy this sense of being lifted as we lift ourselves beyond ourselves, reaching for the greater.

Within the medicine wheel, there are corridors in the four directions. Each represents an aspect of the essence of consciousness. The East is the mental, the South is the emotional, the West is the physical, and the North is the spiritual, and at the Center of the wheel is the heart.

Everything works in cycles, or in a circle, because every circle is the seed of new beginnings. For instance, we have 365 days in which the earth travels around the sun so we can say it takes 365 days for one calendar year to take place around a circle. There is a natural way that the earth revolves. The seasons, for example, are revolving on that same pattern. Springtime, summertime, autumn time, and wintertime complete one annual cycle. Vibration also evolves in a natural order and is continually moving from East (mental) toSouth (emotional) to West (physical) to North (spiritual). But it is moving so fast that the process is not always observable. The flash, or the knowing, can appear quite instantaneously like the seed of a new visionary experience or flash of light.

To explain further. Inherent in the medicine wheel is a five-step process that Nature gives us to make decisions. Sometimes, the entire five-step process occurs in a split second. Other times, we get stuck — for months even — at some place within the medicine wheel. By understanding more clearly that five step-process contained within the very essence of the medicine wheel, we can see where we are stuck on a particular issue, or where we are stuck within our lives as a whole. Then we can take the steps necessary to free ourselves.

The direction of the East, the mental, number one on the wheel, is the direction where there is unity in all things. Then we go to the South, the emotional, which then becomes step number two, where we deal with polarities or opposites, like hot and cold or male and female. Then we move to the West, the physical, step three, the place of reconciliation of the opposites. Then to the North, the spiritual, step number four, where one finds direction and purpose. Finally, one comes to the Center, step five, which completes the circle and is the place of transformational possibilities.

Using this process for decision-making or for the purpose of resolving problems allows the free flow of the decision-making process, because the focus is on process, and not the decision itself, or its outcome.

To use the medicine wheel effectively we must understand not only the five-step process, but also the dominant sound vibrations which are associated with each direction. There are five dominant sound vibrations which give sustenance to the soul. They are the five key vowel sounds: ah, eh, eee, oh, and uu (A, E, I, O, and U, as pronounced in Spanish). The vowel sounds connect us to the spirit world; the consonants connect us to the relative, to placement in physical world. Vowels are spirit and consonants are direction. Each specific vowel sound carries a special quality. And each vowel has a designated place within the medicine wheel.

Mysteries of the East

The sound for the direction of the East on the medicine wheel is the vowel A, pronounced according to the Spanish pronunciation of A, "aah."

"Aah" stands for purification. According to ancient sounds of nature the typology "aah" is "to wash." Try running your shower and listen to the sound that falling water makes and you will hear it sounding "aah." Historically, water has been used in ceremonies for purification and baptism. We know, for example, that Jesus washed the feet of the disciples, Catholics use Holy Water to make the sign of the cross, and water is used for baptism, whether it be a ceremony in which the water is sprinkled or a ceremony of total immersion.

"Aah" is talking about the physical washing as well as the spiritual washing so that's where we get the principle idea of baptism. The Spirit of Water knew that the real reason for baptism is to take people out of the ever-changing world, back to before the time they were born, to the void, the place without thought. In the prehistoric traditions, when children were born, they were given water to drink. Water is put on newborns' hands, on their feet, on their foreheads and on their heads to honor the principal ideas that make up the profile of life and to signify that all of life comes from the ever-unfolding flower of perpetual light.

In some traditions, newborns are given water from hot springs during the ceremony commemorating birth. Spring water brings forth magnetic energy, the vibrancy of the spirit Earth's heart center. This spirit energy is running away from its own resonance that it might know itself by hearing its echoes. Warmth means the arrow of Cupid. When this warm water light is given to "chi" (as in the word child) in baptism, or at the moment that the baby is born, the child's cold truth of chi, of winter time, is initiated into the warmth, the sacred, loving, ever-flowing essence of God's heart, the center of Great-All-Mystery.

Water is used in purification ceremonies of all kinds because it is light, both physical light and spiritual light, that is emanating in all forms. When you look up into the clouds, you see a physical form created by the interaction of light and water. You might see a large, white puff surrounded by a clear blue sky. On the physical level, what is happening is that light is heating the water, causing it to vaporize and coalesce, an action which then bends and reflects the light, making the visible form of the cloud. In a sense, a cloud is not a physical thing, but is the visible manifestation of the union of water and light. But when you perceive the spiritual vibration of that cloud, you perceive yet another reality. In the clouds are "water beings." To the spiritual eye, they look like miniature human beings. They are really angelic beings, known as the "water beings," spirits of water. They are the spiritual light that I am referring to, and the clouds come to the earth as water and we drink them in. As we drink the water from the clouds, we bring into ourselves the spiritual blessings of the water beings, and we become those blessings.

The direction of the East is where the sun rises just like an idea does. It appears and gives us its light. Since water is a metaphor for the light in ideas, ideas wash us with the water from their rivers of out-flowing sunlight. When I was growing up, we would go to the stream to wash ourselves, or we would wash ourselves in a basin of water, but the metaphor alongside my experiences was always the same. What was being enacted in the physical act of washing was the Great Mystery, saying that life was emptiness full of perpetual purity.

The color of the East on the medicine wheel for me became yellow because that is how I saw it. The golden light would open me up to wisdom. I used to have difficulty learning and remembering things. I would open my physical eyes and drink the yellow-gold light. It helped me to stay open to receive and to learn how to remember wisdom. I saw yellow as the doorway of this reality we live in called the house of the ever-shattering light.

For me the East became where wisdom first enters into the conscious essence of an idea. As the first position in the medicine wheel, it is the place where we experience unity. In this place we consider the wholeness of things; we look at a whole tree, rather than its parts; it is here that we get an overview of a situation, rather than focusing on any one aspect. Similarly, we are made to be just like them, principal ideas that are reaching out for their own highest goodness; we begin reaching out for our own highest goodness.

Mysteries of the South

The sound for the direction of the South on the medicine wheel became for me the vowel sound "eh" (pronounced according to the Spanish E).

"Eh" stands for relationship. It is here we learn to deal with all our relationships in life. Ultimately, it is here where we understand our relationship with Spirit from the beginning and forever more. The color of the South in the medicine wheel is white, metaphor for the connection that all frequencies have with each other.

"Eh" in Tiwa means "you," and "you" means "where the physical and spiritual planes come together in innocence in God's carrying light." In the sundance ceremony, a tradition committed to authentic vision, the sun comes down from the sky and dances for three days in order to receive Grandmother Earth's spiritual blessings. The "eh" sound vibration depicts how relativity is the connection bonding all things into the web of life. All things are connected.

The "y" in the English word "you" is pronounced "eee." This sound is the gate of awareness that bonds or connects as in a grid the physical world and the spiritual world of ideas. So, symbolically, when I say "you" I am saying that, at that moment, you are the doorway for me to evolve to my place of higher spiritual awareness. This is one of the mysteries of what life is about, because I found out it takes another person to make me a possibility. I need another person to reflect back to me my identity as it emerges from potential into manifestation. Also, when two people are in relationship to each other, these two sets of vibrations begin to hit against each other, and in that interaction both are changed and lifted. So the "eee" sound in "you" recognizes that other person as a doorway for me, and the "uu" in "you" recognizes that the relationship we are forming is a container in which both of our energies are to be carried, like a glass carries water, to nurture the soul of each of us. The word for soul in Tiwa means "drinker;" the soul is that in us which thirsts for knowledge or truth or enlightenment (or actual water, for that matter!).

Then take "uu-eee." This sound combination in English means "we." In French it is "oui" — "yes." In Tiwa it has two meanings, "to climb," and "to give." All of these ideas spring from a sound combination which encompasses them all. As soon as an English-speaking person says "we," at that moment, he is also saying "to give," "to climb," and "yes." The "uu-eee" vibration moves us to higher consciousness in the same way we are moved up when we give away what we have in order to receive. At the same time it affirms (says "yes" to) our relationship, recognizing that, as many people come together, we are all lifted.

The fastest way to achieve higher consciousness in the beginning of creation was for many ideas, no matter how diverse they were, to come together and to be in a relationship with one another. Nature does not have a name for the vibration of "upward mobility," nor does it have a name for "many people." It only has a name for "going up," and accordingly, "many people" and "going up" are synonymous. So if we belong to a large planetary family as a body of people living together on Planet Earth, we are automatically going to achieve higher consciousness faster because we are made up of many ideas in a relationship with that of community. We came together here because we wanted to evolve beyond the ordinary life we were living as individuals. The "groupness" and the "going-upness" of life is how, in the resonance of vibration, we evolve.

"The people" means "vibration" and represents life on the skin of Grandmother Earth. Because we live on her skin, we automatically are destined to evolve to higher forms, because "skin" or "vibration" is synonymous with "liftingness." So we are automatically being lifted just because we are on the skin of the earth which is made of ideas that are being cultivated and integrated into new designs by Mother Nature.

The position of the South on the medicine wheel also represents the emotional body. Emotional awareness is awareness of feelings. The "eh" sound shows the relationship between one aspect and another aspect, between differences, even the differences of one person from another. The "eh" of South is your relationship with your lover, your relationship with the all the people in your life, the invisible as well as the visible. The South is for the purpose of carrying one another in a loving way. Think of yourself as a single idea resonating so that instead of the whole tree, you see the limbs or the trunk; or, in a situation, you focus on a particular point of view, rather than an overview. What can happen is you may get stuck in duality, in judgment or confusion, or in an inability to decide because you are in a state of separation from your true self. From the South, you jump to reconciliation (the West). It is the nature of vibration for this to naturally occur, and from reconciliation we move to our spiritual purpose in life (North), and next, into transformational potential (Center).

Mysteries of the West

In the direction of the West is the vowel I, pronounced according to the Spanish pronunciation of "eee." "Eee" is the sound of awareness, the vibration of awareness. Awareness is when I understand that inside of self is the place from which insight comes into consciousness.

The metaphor of the Corn Maiden (who is, in our myths, the Field of Dreams) explains the concept of awareness: A young Indian woman stands confidently in a corn field. The gentle breath of the Infinite blows a few loose strands of her silken long, black, braided hair of the Infinite Void. Her graceful body is clothed in the muted tones of buckskin; of the cover of wisdom it is made. A necklace is fastened around her neck, made of intricate bead work and glistening silver; this is the place of the upper and middle worlds. On her feet are a pair of carefully hand-stitched moccasins, made of descending light, which are tied neatly with strips of rawhide, made of perpetual vigilance. In her hand she holds a planting stick, sharply pointed on one end. Her eyes turn downward and she examines the soil beneath, over which water now flows. She bends, ever so slightly, and with her stick probes the earth.

The woman is the symbol of *co weh*, the vibration that brings everything beautiful together in one place. It brings together the North, the South, the East, and the West, the up above, and the down below. The dress she wears is *oh oh nee*, insight, the capacity to hear the sounds of innocence that come into constant review. The necklace is the metaphor of the connection between the earth and the sky, of connecting thinking with feeling. She looks at water, the crystallized light but also heart serum, that which comes from the sacred heart of the innermost place of enlightenment of God's greatness. Because the stick has a point, the moment she pokes it into the soil, she penetrates wisdom, which is ready to erupt and flood forth with awareness.

She stands truly in our awareness of a cornfield of dreams. She stands among the corn stalks of our awareness and she is standing as the metaphor of the awareness of the presence of the Great Mystery. She stands on the awareness of the landscape of the infinite self and allows herself to be drunk through the feet of young women.

And the poet says, "Oh, how beautiful it is to ascend as woman and to stand while sinking into the field of dreams among the corn stalks of her delight."

The direction of the West on the medicine wheel is the direction of the physical. The reason everything became physical is because it wanted to become the concrete form of calling. Calling was and is the process of awareness coming into being. In Tiwa teachings, as soon as a thought is crystallized, it automatically begins to call more of its own kind into existence. Even when we don't speak our thoughts, this tendency of a thought to multiply itself causes our ideas to go out, so that others pick up on them and use them, even if they aren't conscious of doing so. Our thoughts become a part of the outer landscape. Thoughts, like people, places, and things, once they are alive, seek perpetuity; they seek to continue on. Thus formlessness resonates into form through calling. Physicality derives from the resonating form of formlessness. In the West direction, we become aware of calling, and of physicality and concreteness.

The physical body's reason for being is that it wanted to bond faith (the mother/father of the awareness of purity), time, and the ladder to the heavens. That is what created the physical plane. The moment the physical plane was created there was the form of calling, aware of itself.

As the third position on the medicine wheel, the West is where we resolve the opposites and the paradoxes, where we find the solution. It is here that we come into harmony. The reason why we can reconcile is because we disappear and reappear again. This is one of the basic truths of physicality: We flash in and out of existence, but it is happening so fast that it is not apparent to us. Our perception creates a veil around those moments in which we don't exist. In the direction of the West, we are dying and we are birthing. We are the beginning, and we are the end results, and we are everything in between.

Mysteries of the North

The vibrational sound for the direction of the North on the medicine wheel is O, which is pronounced according to the Spanish O, "oh."

"Oh" means innocence, placement, clarity about who you are or what your next step is. It is a level of consciousness that does not have interruption, a state of ascending spiritual continuity. It is the place of the pillar of truth.

"Oh" means child; it means innocence. The vibration of "oh" is constantly renewing itself; it is totally open to the process of evolving, of unfolding. A growing person has the capacity to be open, and has an essence of curiosity which is a free-flowing, constantly renewing selfness — a selfness renewed by experiencing the moments that take it reaching beyond self.

In the direction of the North is the winter, from which all things appear on the wheel of life. We are the O, meaning that we are like the child whose father/mother is standing in the North lifting us higher and higher into life, the child that is born with a purpose and knows where it is going. The North direction (like all the directions) is continually occurring because the medicine wheel only lasts for a moment and then it disappears and then it is born again and then it disappears again. North is the life of all things going through a hollow bone like the hollow bone of the Sun Dancer. And each time life appears and disappears in the direction of the North, there is inno-cence, the ascension of living breath. There is a new being every time. Energy disappears and reappears, and when it comes back it is a new form; even though it may have the same characteristics, it is not the same.

"O" also means placement. To see a chief in his

headdress is to understand placement, even if it is only at an unconscious level. "Chief" means 'chi' or truth, the cutting edge, or the "cold truth." The image of the chief centers everything, just as does the presence of the king. He is at the center of his kingdom. There is the sense that wherever he moves he carries truth and keeps his placement. The chief knows his place. In his presence we are automatically more connected with our own center and our placement in life. The center/chief essence moves us by virtue of its being clearly defined.

The feathers in the headdress worn by the chief mother/father person symbolize the deepest meaning of the vowel "O" — placement — which is really a level of consciousness that does not have interruption, a state of perpetual continuity. On the feathers, the *qui wah* of initiation on the headdress, the first band of color is white, symbolizing all colors of the aura. All colors of all things or moments must be initiated before they can express essence. This is the way of vibration and the color white initiates all the other colors to produce their own particular resonance. Next, is the band of black, *po neh nee*, raw wisdom. The final band extending outward, constantly renewing itself and unfolding, is white again. In wearing the headdress, the chief commemorates this power. Its energy is returned to him through the headdress and is radiated to all in his presence. This is the real reason kings and queens wear crowns. Behind a tradition we can always find a principle idea represented, the purpose of which is the unfolding of consciousness. It is important for the unfolding of consciousness that the forms of chiefship, queenship, or kingship be maintained.

There is a well founded theory in social science that all prehistoric societies saw themselves as being at the center of their universe. Their world perspective was from their position at the center of the circle, with the rest of the world surrounding them. The quality point at the center of the circle is the "Caller of Highest Greatness." One of its inherent qualities that sits at the center of all of life is that it calls greatness into existence for its own personal unfolding. No matter what our view of ourselves is, our consciousness is at the center. Because it is, we automatically attract greatness. That is the nature of vibration. We attract to ourselves the highest potential for that moment, and with it comes a sense of awe for all of life.

So why don't people manifest more greatness? We don't because we have a block in our medicine wheel, a mental, emotional, physical or spiritual block in regard to a particular issue. There may be a mental block, for instance, holding onto a belief such as, "To be poor is noble. It brings you closer to God." And so poverty is what we manifest.

The North is the direction of the spiritual on the circle of life. The spiritual blowing through the circle, through the hollow bone, gives breath to everything. It allows for metaphors to speak and allows for ideas to talk about themselves from inside of the hollow bone, the wall of which is innocence.

The North is also the fourth position on the wheel and is the place where we know our path and know our next step. It is appropriate, then that the color of the North is red, which means completion.

Mysteries from the Center of the Medicine Wheel

The vibrational sound for the center of the medicine wheel is U, pronounced according to the Spanish U (uu).

U means carrying. It speaks of how God is carrying all of life as ideas that are constantly appearing as insights. The human is a medicine bag. A medicine bag contains articles deemed sacred and holy by the person to whom the bag belongs. So it is with us. We carry holy 'objects' in our psyche. The vibration of the sacred medicine bag is to see, to have capacities of the visionary. So, when we carry these forms, we carry the capacity of drinking the light, of being visionaries, exploring existence.

In the center of the medicine wheel is a very empty place. For example, the traditional form for vision quest was to go up to the top of a mountain. Going to the top of the mountain, or the top of any high place, has the quality, symbolically, of going to the heart center of vibration, where we search for not just ordinary awareness but for the highest possibility in conscious awareness. The mountain top is in the environment for the highest potential because the vibration of light there is of a very high quality. It is on the top of a vision quest mountain where heart and mind are bonded together.

The intent of the vision quester is to go to the heart center of the Great Spirit, to the heart of the Great

Mystery, because that is where everything dies into greatness of meaning. The reason Spirit communicates with us at this level is because technically we do not exist. Only in the place of emptiness at the center of life do we gain complete clarity and become aware of the truth, for here we truly are full of nothing, part of all of existence, which is full of nothing.

One of the qualities that energy has is physicality. Because of this, energy awakens the physical body to connect to the mental body, to the emotional body, and to the spiritual body of the vision quester. As soon as all of those four bodies, or four directions, are bonded, the East/mental, the South/emotional, the West/physical, and the North/spiritual, then one enters the above/below and the middle heart level, the fifth dimensional vibration or place. It is in this sacred space that one receives insight and becomes clairvoyant. Only here are we are empty so that we can see into the future and into the past. Technically we do not exist.

Another quality of the center of the circle is that this high clarity connects us with time. I am talking about linear time, and linear time is measurable time. Measurable time comes from the archetype of "traveling goodness." It connects us with this heart center, the heart center of wisdom, which is at the top of the mountain. The heart and wisdom and time are connection for us. We are connected with them when we place ourselves at the top of this highest mountain which is made up of vibration composed of slowed down light that has crystallized into meaning. This crystallized meaning comes from the land and the sky. Vibration reflects from itself new insights in each moment, because light is constantly evolving and growing and needs new insightfulness to grow. It is in our nature to behave this way because we too have our heart, wisdom, and time connection.

The place at the top of the mountain, then, is the place where we are capable of the very highest awareness. Here is transformational potential which sits in the fifth position, at the center of the Wheel of Life. That transformational energy is what we want to experience every single day. In whatever work we are doing, we should say to ourselves, "I would like to tap into that transformational potential today in regard to this particular work I am doing. Work and worship and paying attention is opening myself to highest awareness. I am opening myself for the Spirit of Life to come work with me because this is where the potential for new insight exists." The potential for new insight comes in the act of asking for help from the primary potential of the Spirit, the vibration behind the vibration, which is the basis for vibration, the vibration that comes from the silence of emptiness into crystallized meaning.

Ceremonies with Color

There are many ways to work with the medicine wheel. What is given here are ceremonies using the vibrational essence of color in conjunction with the medicine wheel. I have received these from my own work with "paying attention" spirit.

In this chapter we have given four different colors, one for each direction of the medicine wheel. Different societies, or different clans, might assign other colors for the four directions because of their particular area of interest or concern, so the colors will vary.

It is believed by many writers that the tribes appeared

on the surface of the earth with different mandates. They came here to expand on specific areas of concern. For instance, the Hopis came here to bring prophecy. Other tribes came specifically to present other gifts to the world cultures. Different cultures bring to the planet different ideas for specific reasons, in accordance with assignments which were given to them from ancient times. What is important in today's society is not what is right or what is wrong, but in what way is this unity of the planet manifesting itself. There is only one direction, and that is the direction of "*waa-chi-chi-hu*," the search for becoming. We become the truth that is found in the different colors in order to investigate them, to find meaning. Otherwise we do not exist. Meaning means "Goodness that is purifying the personal self — as above, so below."

Each color has a predominant resonating vibration which, when used in the ceremonies given here, will almost instantly give answers. This is because the color is directly connected to a particular vibration that, when used properly, will connect the brain almost instantly to that which it seeks to know. I first learned this way while I was in the desert without food or water for eight days.

I went out in the desert to fast because I wanted to confront temptation. I took with me a canteen of water and some food, but my intention was to go without food and water for eight days. During the first few days in the desert, I struggled with thirst, but I wasn't really tempted to break the fast. I also stuggled with the heat of the daytime and the cold of the night. Then, after a few days, I ceased to be aware of thirst and heat and cold. I became aware of vibrations from the sand and the plants around me. I noticed that each of these had their own specific qualities of vibration, their own natural resonances.

I then became aware of the vibrations of colors, vibrations not audible, but sensible. They were finer, softer, yet stronger resonances than the normal sounds one hears with the physical ears.

One of the ways to use the medicine wheel is as a preparation for ceremony. Face the East, and purify yourself with the sound "aah." Turn to the West and repeat the sound "eee" to bond you with all things and all of the eternities and to connect you to the physicality of all things in that moment. Face now the direction of the South and sound "eh" that you may be related to yourself and to others. Turn to the North and sound "oh" to connect you to spirit, the breath of everything.

Having called in the four directions, you are now ready to proceed with these or any other ceremonies.

Black Light

In the essence of the darkness is "to call into existence from non-existence that which we are searching for." That is the metaphor of the nighttime. The breath and blackness are the same thing because Spirit is in the breath of nighttimeness. Spirit gives life through the breath to the body of life. Since the breath is what gives life to everything moment by moment, then it is by looking into the black moonlight that we find what we cannot find in the white daylight. The reason we cannot find it in the white light is because what is in the black hasn't appeared yet, hasn't manifested yet. In the white light we do not exist until the dark moonlight gives us existence.

If you want to find out something you know nothing about, formulate a screen in front of you and look into the black light. You may see whatever knowing you are given coming out of the black light, because the essence of black light is seeing that which we have been looking for and haven't found yet. Suppose we want to find out something about someone's health. We send out that seeking vibration, into the black light. Knowledge appears always from the no-formness of the dark space into the white daylight of knowing.

Yellow Light

See again a circle of light. Only this time see the circle as the color yellow because yellow is the symbol of openness — openness to another realm that you have not been able to access up to this point. Create a yellow screen and stare into it. New awareness will open up for you in that direction.

White Light

White light is used to break a pattern or readjust something in your life. For example, you may want to break a mental block or an emotional block of some kind.

Visualize a white screen. See that pattern being shattered and see how you want to remold yourself. If you can visualize clearly on the white light background, then that shift can be made.

Red Light

If you want a satisfactory completion to a task, use the color red as the background on the screen. Put one of your projects up against the red screen. By using the vibration of red, visualize a good ending to that particular project in your life.

Remember that in the beginning we came into existence from a flash of light and it became the first circle that included all of life. Indeed today we are still made up of unfolding moments of appearing and disappearing circles of cognizance, of knowingness. A prayer I use today is: "I love you, my beingness made of awe — my circle of illumination — my circle of life."

CHAPTER FOUR

The MYSTERIES
OF CHANTING

Chanting

Chanting is how we enter into the eternal now. The energetic vibrations of our voices bond us to the spiritual light made of memory, and of now, and of future, for we are the light of universal intelligence. As we chant the Universe speaks to us in metaphoric images.

Chanting calls the pasts and the future into the eternal now. Mother Nature does not have a word for chanting, but it does have a word for now. The Spirit of Now, its resonance, is what is creating the meaning of now. The here and now is the only place on the continuum we can access the future or the past. In fact, we can heal the future even before it needs healing and we can heal the past even though we didn't get to heal it then. We can heal it through the Now by chanting. Chanting is a way of making our past wrongs right, whether these wrongs are imagined, or real, personal or planetary. In fact, the act of chanting and Now were created with the same resonance so that we "the people" could have the ability of analysis.

When chanting or singing, the physical body experiences the essence of each word through the electricity, or light, created by sound. The ancient mystics practiced chanting to stay focused on the here and now. They also used chanting to heal the physical body, and to wash and heal the inner regions of Cosmic Thought. Hildebard of Bingen, a 17th century mystic, once said that when we sing words, their true meaning is revealed directly to the soul through bodily vibration.

Metaphor of the Chanter

The chanter is the cosmic universe in miniature. The person chanting is the embodiment of the earth and sky. When chanting, I start by pretending the in-breath is the sky energy, and the out-breath is the earth energy. The highest nerve center is located at the voice center, the place in the human anatomy where the sky and earth in the human anatomy are connected. Sound vibration connects the mind, body, and spirit, and makes the physical body whole.

In chanting, the areas above the neck of the chanter are designated as sky energies: the eyes, nose, ears, mouth, hair, lips, eyebrows, head, facial skin, teeth, and tongue. According to the ancients, the extension of the feminine is the masculine; another way of stating this is that which descends is female and when it lands on the floor it becomes male. So in chanting, both feminine and masculine energies are involved. The feminine, brings down from higher mind the sustenance of sound; and the male then expresses sound.

Incongruences in the physical body or in the earth, can be attributed directly to our thoughts or voices. Chanting contributes toward healing because it brings into alignment the physical, emotional, mental, and spiritual bodies. It aligns them and integrates them into the here and now because past memory and future are healing as chanting is being done. Chanting is the same as prayers for good health. As the chanter comes into alignment, the earth (as metaphor for self) is brought into alignment as well.

With chanting, the repeated sounds of the consonants direct the power of the vowels in such a way as to create an energy design. Vibration impacts the physical body, bounces back, and on its return, the original form has changed into a new form. Next, as it once again bounces on the newly formed body, it designates the extent of the growth achieved and connects that change with the self.

The vibratory essence of sound affects the inner walls of the nerves and the blood vessels. The inner walls of each cell resonate and the power of vibration (sound) affects not only the physical cell walls but also the mental, emotional, or spiritual walls, zoning "in" or zoning "out" attitudes imposed by values or belief system. Chanting implants in the psyche the basis for the new and fine-tunes the physical body for both spiritual and mental growth.

Preparation for Chanting

Chanting has been done by many different cultures all over the world. Many different forms of chanting have evolved over the centuries by different peoples. Each form has value and each form of chanting is done for the purpose of reaching specific goals. The form of chanting given in this book is a result of my years of study with sound and vibration.

Chanting can be done anywhere. One's preference for chanting in the privacy of one's home, or chanting in a room full of people, or chanting in a sound chamber is perhaps not so important as the intent in the heart of the one who chants. What will be given here is an explanation of how to chant, first using vowels only and then using vowels and consonants. In addition, specific chants for special purposes will be included.

The simplest way to prepare for chanting is to sit upright in a comfortable position, close your eyes, and breath in and out several times to relax the body.

If you are in a sound chamber or wish to use the imagery of the sound chamber, use the following process:

Imagine the sound chamber in your mind. The chamber is the metaphor of the physical body.

Visualize first the feet. Imagine them as your connection with eternal time. Identify yourself with this space.

Second, imagine the floor of the chamber or room as your legs. The area of the legs or floor is the metaphor for greatness on the journey of life.

Third, see the walls or imagine them as your potential for personal growth. The walls are where we make the soul connection.

Fourth, view space in the room as the abdomen, solar plexus, chest, arms, hands, and the back of the body.

Fifth, imagine the ceiling as the neck and face.

Sixth, concentrate on the area above your head.

Seventh, imagine a shrine at the center of the room or chamber. This is the heart center.

How to Chant

Decide what the focus of your chant is to be. Select a word in the English language and chant the word, concentrating on the sound of the vowels from the word. There is an important distinction to be made here. It is not how the vowel in the word might be written that is important, but the sound of the vowel in the word.

For example, if you wanted information on yourself and your name is John, you would chant "jee - aahn," because that is the sound of John. If, your name were Mona, another O word but pronounced differently, you would chant the sound "moh," and in this case, since there are two vowel sounds, the second one, "nahh" would be chanted next. Focus your attention on the whole word as you are chanting its sounds.

Or, suppose a crow flies over your head, and you want to understand the deeper significance of that metaphor appearing. You would focus on the whole word and chant the sound of crow ("keh-row").

If you were going to chant for world peace, you would chant the sound of the word peace, "peeez." Focus on the entire word and chant for twenty to thirty minutes with that intention of supporting or bringing forth world peace. By chanting the sound of the word, "peeez," you would also be calling the presence of the heart connection to mind, body, and spirit as the purifying light.

The vowels in any given word reveal the power of the word while the consonants conduct the power of that energy into a healing current and give it a physical, mental, emotional, or spiritual impulse. The vibration of the vowel sounds enters at the breath level (spirit) and then through the physical level (matter) and then flows (movement) through the body. Thus, we can visualize chanting as the essence of — or metaphor for — spirit becoming form in movement through matter.

As you chant, keep in mind the deeper significance of the vowel sounds as given in the preceding chapter and their placement on the medicine wheel.

A *(aah)* Purification, Direction of the East, Mental Body
E *(eh)* Relationship, Direction of the South, Emotional Body

I *(eee)* Awareness, Direction of the West, Physical Body

O *(oh)* Innocence, Direction of the North, Spiritual Body

U *(uu)* Carrying, Center of the medicine wheel

Please note that vowels have multiple meanings, and that only one is given here.

You will begin to discern other layers of meaning in the various sounds as you chant them. These meanings arise from the vibrations that form the words, and we come to know them through the vibrations we experience as we form the words in our bodies, and through their resonance in the silence that follows.

Sometimes you will need to listen carefully to discern which of the five vowel sounds comes closest to the the way you pronounce the vowel sound in the word you are chanting. This is because English, French, and other languages differentiate more than five vowel sounds. The "short u" sound in the word "up," for instance, might be closest to the "eh" sound for you. In other cases, what we have been taught to think of as one vowel sound, is actually two which are blended. For instance, the "long I" sound in the English word "I" is actually "aah-eee," and the "long A" sound in the English word "day" is acutally "eh-eee."

As you begin chanting the word, visualize a step ladder and place the word on the third rung of the step ladder. The step ladder is used because each rung of the ladder represents a level of consciousness. We begin with the third rung because at the third level is where everything begins to move toward its destination. (The first and second levels are preparatory only. There isn't enough energy in them for forward movement.) Allow the word to climb up the step ladder from the third to the tenth level as you are chanting. Ten in Tiwa thought is the number of completion. In moving the word up seven rungs of the ladder from the third to the tenth, you are also becoming aware of the number seven, which in Tiwa thought speaks of the multiplicity of existence, of the vastness upon vastness upon vastness of levels of consciousness.

Visualize, then, a ladder, and place the resonating word in the empty space above each rung, as it rises from the third to the tenth. Hear the word vibrating in each empty space.

Chanting and the Breath

In vocalizing the sound you are chanting, for example "peeez," hold the "eee" sound for the length of the out-breath and then breathe in and repeat the sound with each slow exhalation for a pre-determined period of time. (The suggested time period is ten to twenty minutes.) Be attentive to insights, such as metaphors that occur to you or images that appear.

When chanting, breathe with the inhalation through the nose and voice the sound as you exhale through the mouth. The inhalation is the metaphor of Father Sky and the exhalation represents Mother Earth. We seek to keep earth and sky and ourselves bonded together and enhance them through chanting. When we chant, we are giving energy to their connection. Historically speaking, separation has led to world unrest, wars, etc., and at a personal level, we feel disconnected because of the lack of connection between earth, sky, and ourselves. The theory is that as we chant our physical bodies into finer atunement, the people living on the earth and the living earth itself will find peace.

Visualize a hollow tree and the wind traveling down the trunk of the tree. The in-breath is bringing in life, and as the wind leaves earth (soul) having touched and fused it with life, it announces the newly created breath of life. *Hu* is outward, carrying, expansion of all life. The incoming and outgoing of the wind (breath) is the spirit of life, the hollow tree is the mind-focus, and the land is "that which drinks the heart resonance of peace to live."

The taking-out and bringing-in actions are to be understood as actions of creator-spirit using humans as a form of creative expression. And so, in chanting, we lose ourselves to the expression of singing.

Chanting Earth Sounds

Tiwa-speaking peoples believe that the physical anatomy of the human being is composed of "*nah*," the Infinite Self. When I say Infinite Self, I am referring to the greater Self beyond the individual or personal self. The Infinite Self is neverending, and each individual person is an aspect of the Infinite Self.

The parts of the human anatomy are metaphors for

parts of the Infinite Self, so that when we chant "nose," for instance, we are exploring the deeper meaning of this one aspect of the Infinite Self, for which the nose is a metaphor. The word for soil in Tiwa is *"nah meh neh"* which is also *"nah"* or Infinite Self, and *"meh"* or goodness and forward movement. (The unaccented *"neh"* sound acts as a stop on the end of the word, like a period at the end of a sentence.) Thus, in Tiwa thought, the names of our body parts are considered earth creativity sounds.

When sounding the earth creativity sounds, you are calling the spirit-intelligence of the word. It is very important to visualize the physical body part as you listen carefully to the word for the body part. The importance in chanting is to become, through sound vibration, the essence of the word and thus to reach the level of ecstasy from which you realize a shift in consciousness.

In chanting, hold the vowel sounds in the word for as long as you can. Consonants can be passed over very quickly or even left out of your chanting, because the vowel sounds are what carry the essence of the word's various levels of meaning. You might begin by chanting the following earth sounds:

Neck – "eh"

Throat – "oh"

Shoulders – "eee oh eh"

Arms – "aah"

Elbows – "eh oh"

Hands – "eh"

Fingers – "ee eh"

Fingernails – "ee eh eh"

Wrists – "eh"

Chest – "eh"

Breasts – "eh"

Stomach – "oh aah"

Hips – "eh"

Skin – "eh"

Knees – "eee"

Back – "aah"

Buttocks – "aah aah"

Legs – "eh"

Feet – "ee"

Ankles – "eh eh"

Toes – "oh uu"

Proceed next to the internal organs. Chanting the

sounds of these organs awakens the innate potential of personal healing power for organs which might be in various states of dissonance and brings about their peace and harmony. Remember that personal healing is also cosmic healing.

> Heart — "aah"
> Blood — "aah"
> Lungs — "aah"
> Liver — "eh eh"
> Ovaries — "oh aah eee"
> Testicles — "eh eee eh"
> Kidneys — "eh eee"
> Pancreas — "eh ee aah"

Sky Sounds

Here are some "above the neck" words to consider next in the chanting process. Note again that in sounding or pronouncing the words, you concentrate on the vowels and keep as close as possible to the sound context as they are used in the word you are studying. As you are chanting remember to visualize the word inside the space above each rung of the stepladder, beginning with the third rung and moving up, allowing the word to climb up to the tenth rung on the ladder, slowly and effortlessly.

Brow — "eh aah uu"

Lips — "eh"

Teeth — "eee"

Face — "eh"

Tongue — "aah eh"

Skin — "eh"

Hair — "eh"

Head — "eh"

Eyes — "aah eee"

Ears — "eee"

Nose — "oh"

Mouth — "aah uu"

Discoveries from Chanting the Elements

Below are some discoveries made from chanting the sounds of the fire, water, wind, land, and wood. The images and metaphors given are just some of the possibilities. If you were to chant these sounds for yourself, you would have your own discoveries to add to these.

The sound of fire is "fahh ehr." By chanting the "aah eh" sound, we investigate the word fire and contemplate the different ways we use fire in our everyday lives. At home we use electricity (fire) in a number of ways. We use electric lights for lighting our homes, gas flames to cook our food, and we use telephones, electric appliances of sorts. The list is endless. All have the base of fire. On clear days, we enjoy sunlight and sometimes on rainy days, a beautiful rainbow made of colored lights. We use fire in a living room fireplace, and we sometimes dine by candlelight. The metabolism of food in our bodies is of fire orientation, as well as our neuro-muscular activity in the physical body. We can say that fire is at the heart and at our roots of survival on the planet. Could we reason that water is also fire?

The sound of water is "wahh tehr." By chanting and humming "aah eh" and visualizing water, one soon is in touch with the wisdom that water can also mean life, purity, and crystallized light. Water is life because it keeps our bodies alive. Without it, life as we understand and know it would soon end. Every time water is taken into the physical body, it cleanses as well as purifies. During ceremonies in which water is used, the essence of water is seen as crystals of light. And yet during an electrical storm, a totally different facet of water can be experienced. Water becomes churning billowing storm clouds. Crystallizing and falling, vaporizing and rising, water particles collide and throw off negative and positive ions, building electrical energy until, in an instant, water becomes fire! With a sudden stroke of immense power, lightening streaks through the air. This transformation from water to fire, taking place at the subatomic level, becomes visible on a giant scale, scorching the air to over sixty thousand degrees within a millisecond of time and sending flames along a jagged path visible for miles. We see it and we are exhilarated and filled with awe.

Lightning lights up the earth and heats the air, firing the wind into action. Chanting the wind sound of "wehnd," the chanter learns that wind can also be equated to fire and water and, like them, has qualities of purification. The combination of water and fire heat creates a force of wind that purifies the earth and sky with cleansing winds, lightning, and rain. The wind pushes clouds from the sky and can blow away an inversion. The wind is the breath of the human lungs. As oxygen in the blood stream, it becomes a mineral and it plays its role in sustaining life.

Chanting the mineral (land), the "eh" sound, the chanter is in touch in an intimate way with the essence of planting, growing, and harvesting, similar to those experiences of the gardener or farmer. The chanter learns that what we sow is what grows. Cultivation of the plants is important in assisting the plants to produce a harvest in abundance. In the metaphor, the corn seed is planted in the soil of the soul. The roots of the seedling are the fire of the sacred heart, the stem is the wood for carrying, and the green of the corn plant is the symbol of trust, of the resonance of "the people," as it reaches forth to touch and become both earth and sky. The corn, as it stands strong and straight, is alive because it is fire, water, air, mineral, and wood.

In chanting the word wood, the "uu" sound, the chanter learns to understand carrying and relationship. Trees grow tall and have strong roots in the land; therefore, they resonate with a sense of placement. Fire and placement are the same in the psyche of Beingness. The next time you walk outside your home and look up at the tree that lives on your street, say to it, "I know now that you are the symbol of greatness and you have been standing still while holding greatness for us so that, when we are ready, we will choose to carry it for you in our lives."

Many trees grow in communities or clusters and give refuge to birds, plants, animals, and humans. Greatness is kept pure by the fire of the heart. Like the tree that sends water to its extremities, Greatness sends breath (wind) of life to the "all," and regeneration to the soul (drinker). Fire, water, air, mineral, and wood are truly one essence. The fire, water, air, mineral (land), and wood are energies that constantly play a role in awakening us to our perceptions of a higher order.

Group Chanting

There are several ways in which groups can come together for the purpose of chanting. A group of women and men might chant in the following way. Ten women begin chanting the designated word sound and then, during their inhalation, ten men chant the word sound so that the continuous sound is sensed and felt by the chanters on the inhalations as well as the exhalations. This is glorification of the Creator Spirit in all humans and in the macrocosm. As the chanter inhales, the Spirit enters into the chanter and gives birth to life. As the chanter exhales, the Spirit of Life and the chanter participate together in generating health and vitality for all things living on earth and in the sky.

Colorado Chanters

During Desert Storm a group of chanters gathered to chant in a sound chamber in Colorado. Any external war exists because there is war within individuals. The metaphors given while chanting with a focus on war would tend to be both personal and collective in nature. A seer was chosen, someone who would be the spokesperson for the group. The sound A (aahh) for purification was chanted five or six rounds, while each person in the group thought about what was going on in the Middle East. The seer reported seeing an enormous spiral of light. When asked what that spiral meant to him, the reply was "liberation." Using the sounds from the word "liberation," the group chanted. The seer reported the following:

"I see a room with dark wooden paneling. In the center is a long, rectangular table. It seems very important, very sacred. There are several high-back wooden chairs around the table. There is a runner on the table made of soft hand woven fabric. There is a sense that this might be England and yet a feeling that this is the sort of table where Jesus sat. I am drawn to a massive door. It is a weathered old double-door made of oak. As I come closer to the door I see a lion's head. In his nose there is a brass door knocker. I feel a strong urge to open the door and step through the doorway."

The metaphor of the doorway is entering. In essence there are only two actions in life, entering or leaving. Since this imagery came from the seer, and so was for the collective whole as well as for each person, everyone was asked to close his or her eyes and to enter the experience by going to the door, opening the door and seeing what awaits on the other side. I report two of those experiences:

"As I approach the doorway, it is with some hesitation. I cautiously place my hand on the doorknob and open slowly. When I open the door the universe is before me. I am overwhelmed with its vastness and beauty. There is a knowing that I need to take a step. At first I hesitate. It seems frightening. I am unsure. I don't know if it will be safe. I don't know where it might lead. My fears start to subside. With all the force from within my being, I step forward. I do not fall. I hear the word 'Abundance.' I am filled with deep emotion. Tears well up from within. I feel supported in a way I have never known."

Powerful images like this one have an impact immediately but usually take some time for their full meaning to unfold and so this same chanter reported back several months later. "I had worked very hard to bring an outside speaker to my area of the country who had a great deal to teach mothers and daughters about bonding and rites of passage into womanhood. I was disappointed when there was not enough support to warrant her coming. When I called her to share the disappointing news, her surprising response was, 'You should teach the course yourself. You have learned a great deal with your own daughter through your own experiences, plus you have studied the Native American ways for some time. And the rest that you think you don't know will be given to you.' I was startled. The universe was offering me an opportunity. I remembered the earlier image from Colorado. It gave me the courage to step forward. I have been amazed at how life has responded. My work is growing and in demand. As promised, I am receiving abundance on all levels."

Another chanter had a different experience:

"I stand before the massive oak door and place my hand on the doorknob. I open the door. I walk into another reality, into another world of perception. There is the delicate beauty of India, lyrical, mystical. I walk into a beautiful courtyard, lush and green. Golden sunshine beams everywhere. In the center of the courtyard is a fountain, one that pours forth liquid light. There is the sense that this is the fountain of life."

The next day this same chanter went to the hot springs in Glenwood Springs, Colorado. The hot springs can be visited by going underground to the caves and then sitting while the steamy vapors of the hot underground springs fill your body with their healing essence. For her, the descent was a treacherous one. Claustrophobia had been her nemesis for some time, so it took great courage to muster the strength to go underground and surrender to the womb of the Mother. When she came up from the underground caves, she went to the designated area to relax. There, in a courtyard-like setting, was that same fountain she had seen in her vision. As a child, she had access to other realities, but had often questioned her experiences. Here was tangible proof of other realities. Her ability to tap into other dimensions no longer needed to be feared, but instead could be accepted as her gift. The fountain seemed to say she was coming to life.

Mysteries of the Consonants

Vowels in any given word reveal the power of the word and the consonants determine the direction the power of the energy must travel. Vowels alone are sufficient for chanting, so it would not be necessary to include consonants. However, a list of consonants and their definitions is included, so that in your word studies, you may have more information about the deeper levels of the vibration of any word.

Again, please note that the consonants have multiple meanings, and only one level of meaning is represented here.

B – head

C – thirst

D – touch

F – faith

G – beauty

H – lifting, unchanging, arms

J – shepherd

K – soul, planting

L – mental, sky and earth connection

M – manifestation

N – self

P – heart

Q – initiation

R – abundance

S – Above/Below, The Beautiful One

T – time

V – drinking, swallowing

W – twice carrying

X – physical power

Y – awareness

Z – above, below

Once you understand the meaning of the vowels and the consonants, then you can do a breakdown of any word and explore other possibilities of meanings. For example, take the word peaceful: *p* – heart, *eee* – awareness, *s* – the Beautiful One (God), *f* – faith, *uu* – carrying, *l* – sky and earth connection. When all the sounds are put together, it translates this way: the heart is aware of the Beautiful One and so in faith carries mind and body as one.

Choose any word, and write by each sound the definition of the vowel and the consonant. Then, write or speak the new definition.

Benefits of Chanting

The moment the spirit breath of life touches the soul, creation occurs and the new form travels out via the mind for ultimate expression and expansion. At that moment, the spirit of life, the spirit of the body, and the spirit of the mind, have bonded into a delightful glorification. It is like a river when a flood of water cuts a new channel through what was once dry land. The river alters and expands. When spirit floods in, the mind expands.

Hence we can say the mind, spirit, and physical body have birthed new territory into higher consciousness.

The vibration of chanting awakens and strengthens the vitality and health of the chanter at the cellular level. Vibration works on the physical and biological aspects of the chanter's being, promoting mental and emotional health. Through chanting, the bombardment of sound (spirit words) acts on the land (physical, biological bodies) in such a way that old forms are lifted out of their former places and raised to new levels.

In the metaphor of the medicine wheel, chanting rapidly cools the vibration, moving us to the place in the vibratory level that defines the "high self-awareness," the cold, winter place. As the cooling of the vibration occurs, new ideas, creations, discoveries, and inventions come out of physical forms and produce the basis for new spiritual vibrations that, in turn, become entities in the warmth of the summer place.

Understanding the Second Level of Language

As mentioned earlier, there are two levels of language. First there is the ordinary language of everyday life. This is the language of the left-brain world, linear, logical, rational. A sentence like "I am going to town" has an obvious meaning. The second level of language is the right brain orientation, the world of intuition, feeling, and spirit. At this level, "I am going to town" has a totally different meaning and carries a different vibration. The sentence becomes a series of sounds. Our original sentence has been transformed into aah-eee eh oh-eee uu aah uu and now means: the purification of awareness has a relationship to innocence that is carrying purification into innocence. The ordinary is transformed into the divine.

Exercise

To practice working with the concept of the second level of language, take an ordinary sentence. Write above it the sounds from each word, referring to the meanings of those sounds given in Chapter Three. Hear the sounds; speak the sounds. Listen for new meaning.

CHAPTER FIVE

VISION OF THE SOUND CHAMBERS

Prayer outlines the direction of our faith and in ceremony we cry out to the infinite that it might let us see with its eyes our own destinies.

Asking for a Vision

Prayer and ceremony have always been an important part of my life. I was taught by my father and my father's people to pray all the time by becoming the being of movement, or speaking, or writing. I was taught that everything is sacred and alive. I was taught to honor all principal ideas by keeping a continual state of prayer with their essences, every single moment of my life.

I asked for a vision which might show me how best to serve the earth and honor all life, to honor walking on the surface of the earth at this time. Then, in the summer of 1983, I received a vision. I had this vision partly because I was trying, through prayer, to keep a connection with the reality that everything is sacred and alive. Also, I came from parenting that trained me for visions. I was told by my parents and grandparents that it was my destiny to have visions. I was taught that life is the visionary unfolding of the Great Mystery, and so, in its image, we too are visionary by nature.

My vision came during a long dance. The Cosmic Mother/Father being came in a flash of light, a point of illumination which lasted only two or three seconds. I cannot begin to explain this vision, it was so beautiful. I then slowed down time and went back into the vision to have another look. In the vision I was shown people praying (directing our faith) and singing (bonding our faith with the present) together in a sacred sound chamber resonating with light. The chamber was an oval structure of mud (matter carrying direction) and straw (ancient knowledge), partly underground (underworld) and partly above ground (middle world). It was a house of the sound of presentness, a structure built to reverberate sound. The melodious chanting of men (essence of expanding light) and women (essence of descending light) were a reflection of people whose spirits and voices resonated in absolute harmony to balance the present, the future and the memory of how the cosmos is oriented through the use of sound.

Everything inside of the house was created by the mirth of the yellow people, light made of truth. The house they created was time that had been slowed down so that we, the people, might seek to know the vastness of our inheritance. The house was made up of many dawns, middays, and moonlit nights. Inside the house lay the principles that would hold and nurture life, that would carry us from dawn to dusk and then take us into beautiful and meaningful dream states, and then beyond them. In the morning time of consciousness, time, again, as was its destiny, would awaken us to what had been discovered in the nighttime for us to hold on to and then to explore.

Beyond the circle of this light, where the walls stood, darkness fell. Light stopped there because beyond would be the "no form place of the breath of revelation." This "no-form place" would also be the place from which all new things could come to be known by the people on their journey to perfection.

In the vision, I was given my task — to build sound chambers around the world. It would seem that, having had this powerful experience, I would have a fearless commitment to honor that clear knowing. What followed, though, was the testing of the commitment, a period of deep self-questioning. Called by whatever name, it was doubt, and doubt stayed with me for some time. And then a reminder came.

An important event needed to occur before I could commit to the vision. This time, it was a waking experience and a woman played the role of initiator. She was probably not aware what role she was playing, but she was an instrument of the divine, nonetheless! On the insistence of this woman, I went to see a particular site, an ancient site near Cortez, Colorado. Here were sound chambers similar to those I had seen in my vision. I was being reminded of my task. Being in those ancient chambers kindled the spark again. Always, there is a symbol before the event. This experience foreshadowed what was to come.

I began looking for somewhere to build a chamber. For several months, I considered various sites, but I couldn't find any land that seemed suitable. Then three months after the original vision, I had another vision.

This time I was in Bernalillo, New Mexico, at my home, and was outside doing ceremony in the sweat lodge. Suddenly, I was taken up to a realm above the clouds, maybe thirty thousand feet or so above the ground, and was faced with a Council of Elders. There were a group of twelve or so wise men draped in red blankets, sitting in a circle. I was asked the question I had been avoiding: "Why have you not built the chambers?" I wanted to elaborate on how I had been busy searching out the right place with just the right environment and how nothing had seemed suitable. Rather than a complicated explanation, which I knew would be unacceptable, I simply said: "I could not find a place." Almost immediately, I was taken and placed next to the sweatlodge and then I looked up and I saw an angelic being descending as a ring of light on a shaft of light, while I heard a voice in the background saying, "We will show you where to build it." The ring of light descended on my garden plot right beside my house. This was where the chamber was to be built. In awe, I watched as a second circle of light appared inside the first. In this circle an angel appeared, holding a child in its arms. The angel placed the baby in the center of the first circle while saying these words: "Now you must raise this child!"

The vision was over in a flash. The site of the original sound chamber had been chosen, not in an isolated area or some beautifully forested mountaintop, but on a site located on a small, dry, flat, strip of land, in a New Mexico trailer park, where simple houses crowd in on both sides, amid the blaring of too-loud stereos, interspersed with the laughter and conversation of day-to-day life, and the occasional clanging of the train as it rumbles past on the nearby railroad tracks. Smiling over it all would be the ever-present face of the Sandia Mountains, metaphor for the Heart of God. It seemed the perfect paradox. The first sound chamber would be built on that ring of light where the angel appeared. And it would be my work, now, to raise that child of light.

The next day I dug up my garden to begin building a chamber in spite of my wife's public contestation. In the vision the sound chamber was an egg-shaped oval built half in and half out of the ground. It would sit where the earth and sky meet, to unite the masculine and feminine. By so doing, it would bring wholeness, harmony, and peace on an inner level to the individual, on a political level to all humanity, and on a cosmic level to the universe. I knew in those moments immediately following the vision that the chamber was the circle of light, and the child had been planted inside the heart that all life everywhere might manifest its goodness. Insights are born similarly.

Purpose of Sound Chambers

To date, some twenty sound chambers have been completed around the globe, including areas as widespread as Australia, Austria, Florida, Pennsylvania, and Colorado. Each of these chambers has its own integrity, purpose, and particular qualities. Each is the result of the committed efforts of a few individuals.

The chambers are our caretakers, helping us to access

wisdom from an ancient source. They act as a mouthpiece for the higher mind to amplify that which we need at this time on the earth and to help all who walk upon her. By building chambers on the surface of the earth, a web of light is created so that a person making sound inside a chamber sets up a continuous resonance around the earth.

We are each made from music. Every one of us was creatively inspired from our dreamtime. Our creator made us from principal ideas or fundamental truths which inhabit and govern the cosmos. Our main purpose in life is to dialogue with the self-empowering qualities of these principal ideas which were instilled in us and in the physical beauty of the earth.

Working as a group, people then become a collective instrument of the resonance of beauty for a particular sound. Each sound chamber would become its own syllable signature because of its placement on the surface of the planet, and each chamber holds a specific purpose. That specific purpose or principle idea would be amplified by the geological and geographical sound particular to each place.

In a chant, the vowels carry the essential meaning or

fundamental truth embedded in each syllable, and the consonants propel, or give form. Like ripples across the lake, the sound waves move out into the earth from each chamber. These waves then open the earth to healing from the ancient sacred places where wisdom has been stored for countless eons.

The visionary child buried in the ground under the first chamber is a symbol of the vision's purpose. At some stage the child will mature and start to teach. I predict the chambers will become active when the child (the vision) reaches the age of twelve. This is the age when Jesus started teaching. It is also the time when social scientists say children become capable of abstract thought. Among my own people, it is the same time when parents must release a child to be trained by the elders and to take his or her place in the collective. Perhaps it is now time for us to let the earth go and let it grow on its own rather than us controlling it as if it were our child, and we were refusing to let it go.

The third and final part of the vision has yet to be revealed. This part of the vision will show us what the sound chambers are beyond the beyond.

The MYSTERY
OF METAPHOR

My grandfather said, "Become listeningness and you will find the spirit of the
gift of life and it will appear as work."

The mystery of metaphor is the art
of listening to life in the activity of work,
of allowing yourself to be living harmony. Metaphors give
us a way to become more inside our universe. If we can
name, or identify our world, we know better how to fit in
harmony with it. Harmony is the warmth of the heart
slipping through a slice of light. By becoming more
attuned to the vibrations in life, we come closer to our
natural state. We clear our blocks and our resistances. We
discover the power to be.

In this chapter are a number of ideas and terms with a description of the metaphors that accompany these words. The definitions given are mine, my explanation for them. They are the result of my personal exploration and discoveries with sound and vibration, and are given as one of many potential possibilities of what one can discover. They are given to encourage you to become an active participant in your own journey. Make your own discoveries. If there is one definition, there are five. If there are five, there are ten. Don't get stuck in one possibility; find the many possibilities. Use the insights of innocence that own you. Possibilities sneak up on us when we least expect them. The realm of all of the infinities that make up the complexion of our being were created by us in such a way so that they might slip into our consciousness when we would be least prepared for them. Use the insights that are given to you in a way that will enhance you and your life. Enjoy your exploration. Fall in love with life! The spirit of the "awe" in life is created when we combine "purity and descending light that is reflective."

Metaphors of the Body

When Mother/Father Creator Spirit made the first humans, Creator made their heads from direction of sacred vibrations. Creator made their heads with the "Spirit of Direction of Focus" and with the "Spirit of Direction of the Sacred Path." Creator in that moment made the focus and the sacred path of the cosmos, for they were both made of reflective light of the Godhead. The Creator made:

Their *faces* with the "Spirit of Entering" that all the eternities would be open to them.

Their *noses* with the "Spirit of Expansion" of places beyond the beyond.

Their *eyes* with the "Spirit of Validation," of imprinting.

Their *mouths* with the "Spirit of Seeing Greatness," for greatness would they be.

Their *ears* with the "Spirit of Giving," to live their work.

Their *hair* with the "Spirit Connection of the Heavens," for communication.

Their *skin* with the "Spirit of Evolution," to lift themselves beyond highest goodness.

Their *necks* with the "Spirit of the Dividing Line Between the Earth and Heavens." The Heavens are the freezing place, home of the story teller.

Next Creator made their bodies:

Their *hands* of the "Spirit of Light" and the "Spirit of Manifesting." From these two spirits came first woman and first man.

Their *arms* of the "Spirit of Lifting," of embracing the heart.

Their *bodies* of the "Spirit of Love," and they were made of Time and Carrying.

Their *legs* of the "Spirit of Movement," that movement might become. Their feet of the "Spirit of Awareness of Self," and the "Spirit of Entering Inwardly," for they would leave trails full of their light because their tracks were wisdom's walk.

Their *knees* of the "Spirit of Completing Cycles."

Their *backs* of the "Spirit of Emptiness."

Their *stomachs* for the "Spirit of Holding Time," that they might be able to stay crystallized before returning beyond the beyond, to Timelessness and no-form.

Metaphors of Postures or Actions

Sitting became Greatness.

Standing became Questing.

Walking became Timelessness walking inside the ice crystals of Truth as it had chosen to be carried by Hu (exhalation).

Holding became the living Truth of The Great Mystery in all things. Carrying became another word for the principle idea of God.

Talking became the Omnipresence, tuning to the cosmos.

Kneeling became to bring the Being of Completion.

Sleep dreaming became the healing present of the vast self beyond duality.

Resting became the living, inner vitality of the self within, bonding with power.

Running became the bonding with all relativities.

Walking slowly became the cosmic heart, the washing, the healing heart.

Walking fast became the hunting aspect of consciousness, of inner awareness.

Thinking became Heart thinking.

Miscellaneous Metaphors

BELLS

The bell sounds are what enter between the slices of light and irrigate light with essence. Bells originate from the idea of insight. Bell means in metaphor, the "strike of light" that slices the ice crystals that are filled with wisdom. Therefore, when we have a new insight, there is a strike of light that occurs. This strike of light carries the sound of the bells. The bell sound carries with it the power to awaken and lift that which it awakens. The bell is that moment when lightning strikes. Whatever it strikes it awakens and gives consciousness. The bell is the best metaphor to use to describe cognizance. When we have cognizance five bells ring out, although we don't always hear the bells. When these five bells, or vibrations, ring out, they imprint in the psyche the idea as vibration. The bell is the call for us to enter into an action that presents us with a potential to move in some given direction.

The bell can open the psyche to a new understanding that comes from the beauty of the Higher Mind that is made up of beyond-the-heavens. The bells bring into consciousness an element of vibration, or energy, that connects the mind to the heart and the heart to the mind. The bell also connects the heart to the periphery of the circle of consciousness. In other words, if we could see a circle of light, the bell is the energy coming from the periphery of the circle of light to the center, or the energy that is going from the center to the periphery of the circle of light simultaneously.

The Land of the Giants

Once when I was plowing fields, I took a break in the late afternoon and lay on my back to rest. My body was warm and there was perspiration on my back. And then I looked up into the sky. I saw two giant beings watching me. I knew that they knew that I had caught them because I imprinted them into my psyche. One stood up and walked away. The other, still watching me, slowly stood up. Still looking down at me, the being hesitated momentarily, then turned and walked away. As he did so, his back disappeared in increments beyond the sky's horizon.

If you want your own experience with the Land of

Giants, pick a late afternoon. Take a long walk first to build up heat in your body and then lie down on your back in a grassy place and watch the sky horizons. Squint your eyes and look for a change in vision, an opening in the sky, so that you will be able to see beyond the physical realities into the ultimate realities. Don't try too hard; don't force it.

DRUMMING

Drumming opens up three basic vibrations. Drumming awakens the self. Drumming heightens the ability of perception, and drumming enables the person to see into the deeper realms of the self.

Drumming, by its very nature, creates a lifting energy which moves you very quickly to the next level of consciousness. That lifting quality is directly connected to the dynamic tension of energy struggling to achieve its highest potential. The sound that comes out of that awakened potential is the manifestation of new idea or a new form.

Drumming creates in the psyche of those people who listen to the drum, a sense of abundance, a feeling that there is more than enough in life to sustain life. There is the feeling of strength, of being able to step forth with whatever one wants to change, because the power to sustain that change is in the drumming. The drumming sound helps persons listen to themselves as they really are.

The kind of skin on the drum determines the kind of energy that is evoked. If the drum is covered with buffalo skin, you are calling buffalo energy; if it is elk skin, you are calling for elk energy; if deer hide, then you are asking for deer energy.

Buffalo energy is the energy of planting, the way energy plants itself onto itself. Elk energy is the energy of that point at which the imprint is created at the level of consciousness by the striking light. Up until that time, nothing is known, but once the imprint is made, that is elk medicine. The deer is the vibration that all the wisdom of all the potential possibilities is knowable. If, for instance, a person wants to open up a connection with a loving soul, or the group loving soul, or the soul of those who have gone before, then buffalo drumming might be used, whereas we would use elk to go to that place where new insights are appearing on the loving blackboard of consciousness, and we would use deer to align the loving of ourselves to infinite wisdom.

It is important to remember the ancient meaning of life and know that everything has meaning. Forms are chosen with preciseness. Metaphors are not mixed, so when we use certain forms, such as a buffalo drum or an elk drum or deer drum, we are doing so to achieve certain results.

Drum Dancing

I was given a vision in which I saw a drum dance. Men and women dancers were moving rhythmically back and forth on an open field from inside a giant drum that was being played. The dancers were moving forward and backward because they were made of mimicking energy that was present in the "Here" (the present), and then in the "There" (the future), and then returning to memory in orientation.

The drum was made from a hollow log with a skin on it. The people who were playing the drum said that when doing a drum dance, the dancers would bring forth greatness because the wood is greatness and is what the drum was made from. The dancers would dance the vibration of the sound, bouncing back (present) and forth (future) and returning to past memory, like the sound waves which were bouncing back and forth inside the hollow log of the drum being played. This would be a way by which all physical life would pick up the resonating vibration of sound by which to shift consciousness. This could create the necessary planetary changes because the planetary energies wanted to dance effortlessly between the present, future, and memory of harmony.

As a result of that vision, drum dances are held annually in the United States, in Europe, and in other places around the world. The way the drum dance works is that dancers dry-fast (drinking and eating nothing) and dance, with intermittent rest periods, for a period of three days. During the first day, the dancers release emotional hindrances to their personal growth, such as anger or grief. By the second day, fatigue starts to set in. As the physical body surrenders, there is, at the same time, a sense of exhilaration, of transcending limitations and beliefs about oneself. The dancers begin to receive glimpses of other parallel realities.

During the third day, a golden plate forms over the heads of the dancers and another plate appears directly below on the ground at the feet of the dancers. From time to time, the energy spirals from the lower plate to the upper plate, connecting the Earth energy with the Sky energy. There is an indentation where each dancer has been standing, which symbolically identifies that dancer's universal placement on his or her path in life.

This vibration of golden light moves upward through each dancer into the atmosphere, where it becomes a ring of light that spreads around the earth. This light, then, is a part of the rain which falls on plant life, on the gardens and the forests, and on animal life. In time, this vibration of greatness gets into the food chain. People eat this vibration in their daily food and begin to experience moments of high essence in their lives.

The drum dance offers an opportunity for those people who want to participate in the consciousness of the planet. In addition to what happens on the collective level, each dancer is uplifted mentally, emotionally, physically, and spiritually.

Flute

The original idea of the flute was that it was the way by which the cycle could be completed between the masculine and the feminine energies. In traditional Native

American practices, the young men would play the flute for the young women in order to keep alive that ancient tradition of the visible calling the invisible. In the playing of the flute, a marriage, or a bond would form and complete the circle of the feminine and the masculine. The feminine starts the energy moving toward the sun and goes part way, and the masculine energy courts the vibration of the lover and brings it back into oneness on the physical plane.

The flute is an instrument connecting the two worlds, the non-physical with the physical. The breath of the flutist is the breath of God coming through a hollow reed; the sound is that of the invisible lover courting the visible lover, the metaphor of the lover and the beloved.

RATTLE

The rattle is how to get in touch with the vibration of "chi." The chi sound in the rattle calls into existence the wisdom that is held in the place of the ice cold plane. When the chi interacts with heat, psychic energy is created. When the cold energy of chi builds to a powerful resonance, it can then explode on contact with heat. At that moment, the potential power is awakened for a higher knowing. Physical heat, which is generated through effort or exertion, is important because as the heat rises in the physical body of a human being and collides with the cold temperature (chi energy), a shift in consciousness is created.

Story Telling

Stories are told in the winter time because stories come from a place of ice, from a place way far away. This place of ice is so far away that it is really present in the eternal now. It is right here where we are and yet it is not here. All of the teachings are frozen in this ice place. Out of this ice place comes the breath, the food that feeds the Creator, the Cosmic Mother- Father. The Creator then proceeds to feed the Spirit of the action being of Cosmic Consciousness.

In this storage place made of ice sit all of the principal ideas. It is said that when stories are told in the wintertime, the ice melts with each story that is told. The water that melts from this frozen place is full of ideas. When this light, which is the water that drips off this frozen plane, falls like rain in tiny little droplets onto the mind of all living things on the planet, it fuses ideas with the mind. It endows the mind with the life giving energy of chi. And when the physical beings of all levels — the plant beings or the tree beings or the human beings or the four-legged beings — get this ice cold spirit in their psyche, they manifest it through action. That is why work is necessary, to bring that cold light into the physical heat of consciousness, through exercising mentally, emotionally, physically, and spiritually. It is through work that this energy vibration can be manifested into physical forms that can feed the soul of all things.

Eighteen Ideas

Here is a list of some fun ideas to contemplate that represent for me some of the energies of life on the physical plane:

1. Planet Earth is constantly giving life to all things on the earth so that, in the act of giving to us, she shows us all how to serve, to give to her and to ourselves.

2. First was the Dream and then the Vision that became the walking, talking, light of the one Great Mystery, which is all of us who are living on the Earth.

3. *Taah-Keh* , (the Big Bang) was created "to initiate action" and from this came the first circle of light. [*Taah-Keh* refers to a Tiwa myth in which two fawns being pursued by the Old Giantess hide inside the crack in a plow. When Plowmaker hits the plow with his hammer, the fawns go flying out.]

4. The eyes are the channels for the "washing lights" that bring clarity to ideas.

5. The rainbows are the hues (vibrations of the rock people) of life on the earth. And the rainbows represent, in metaphor, the breath of the Butterfly of the Dream Time, the bridge to eternity.

6. The Earth is the Mother Starship of the Ancient Ones.

7. Resonating energy is simply universal intelligence descending onto its own understanding of the vast greatness of its own greater, inner self.

8. The idea of enteringness created the first form of the face.

9. Water is crystallized light which produces physical light as well as spiritual light. Interestingly, the symbol for water in chemistry is H_2O. In Tiwa the sound of HO,

"*Haah-Oo*," means "Little Leaf." The leaf is the symbol for life.

10. From the first mist of the first cloud comes the idea of birthing as dropping from the biological mother's womb. And the thread that keeps us connected to our origins was primarily created to help us keep vigilance over what we do and say: right actions/right thoughts.

11. Life on the earth is a living daily experience of inspiring qualities and inner knowing. We find them, these gems of truth, only as we are ready to acknowledge them in our own lives.

12. The light is always chasing the shadow and the shadow is always following the light.

13. The breath is the key to all of the mysteries.

14. The breath is the infinite void from which all creativity is first given life, then its purpose.

15. Dream essence of life is what heals life, whereas living life is the visionary part of it.

16. The first visionary who came from the first dream was in the dream state too because he was dreaming his vision. That is, he was the dreamer and the one being dreamed. Consequently, all of life is simply made up of a

healing state that is dreaming itself beyond itself.

17. The eyes are how the Great Mystery sees, how it holds on, moment by moment holds to the gifts of each moment before the next moment appears, bringing with it its own face.

18. The earth is a large stone which is the holder and keeper of all of the mysteries that created the life potential here on the earthly home of the People.

Having read these ideas, go outside and sit on a rock that has been heated by the sun. As you sit on the stone, the warmth of the rock will travel through all parts of your body and when the radiant heat from the stone has traveled through all the different parts of your body, the knowledge that lives in what you have just read will be acknowledged and will appear in your life. Hereafter, you will get greater clarity on these principles.

CHAPTER SEVEN

FREEDOM
FROM CHOICE

 My hope in writing this book is to help
people live in freedom from choice, in a
state of grace, following that path of
impeccability which we chose for ourselves before we came here. As we pulsate
between formlessness and form, we receive insight. We
remember, suddenly, what we chose for ourselves in the
time before time. Following that insight, we give energy to
the form of our highest good, and this movement becomes
natural for us, involuntary, like breathing. We are freed
from doubt, from the choice of the ego, into a way of being
in harmony with the Higher Mind.

The Vibration of Time

Time purifies itself by calling into existence conceptual abstract forms from the "No-Form Place" and creates them into crystallized images in order to observe its own personal beauty.

First, there was only the dark infinite void. In the beginning there came the being of calling, of divine longing, and God called forth the light. When that happened, time began to form as one part descending light, one part ascending light. Then, manifestation was made of one part descending light and three parts ascending light. Then, relativity was created of three parts descending light and one part ascending light.

But before time could become the reflective universe, the Great Farmer created a place for emergence. I saw it in a vision of how *waah-maah-chi* made cosmic consciousness. I saw that we, the people, are the vibration of God's planting field of *naah peee aah neh* and the planting field is God's plan for us here on the Earth. The Earth is the clay we are made from, from which God raises his spiritual crops.

The fertilizer of God's planting field (us) is firstly made of the eternal flame that feeds our essence of *gaah - weh*, of "all our relations," our union with all that is. Because we are rooted in the soil, fertilized by the flame, we become the flame of consciousness for the Infinite Self. Thus, God places us as the eternal flame into the soil of the highest order of self. Secondly, it, the planting field, opens the doorway for the people to ascend as we evolve on into higher consciousness (i.e. higher planes). Thirdly, through the action of movement, through work (which is worship), the planting field allows our personal growth as individuals.

The Flash of Light

The flash of light in which I perceived my visions became the flesh on the forms that I saw, whereas what was contained in the visions themselves were the insights embodied in them. In another way of speaking, the flash of light gave me the opportunity to see in an instant a lot of formulated wisdom, and in that same moment I was granted the gift of becoming its inner meaning. Visions seem to work that way.

Growing up at Picuris, I remember the teaching that the farmer is the being of *oh - kaa - meh - eh*, "the essence of childlike innocence of the highest goodness that sits." Therefore, in the action of the farmer planting the fields, he brings into the field, as he prepares and then plants it, the essence of his own being. In the season of springtime the Cosmic Mother/Farmer prepares the soil with childlike innocence of the highest goodness. Innocence sits and blesses the land just planted with that specific essence. The farmer, in the action of planting, awakens the ancient memory of the field in us. The field, which is now awakened, can follow its natural course of awakening the seeds that have just been planted there, to sprout them and so to bring forth their life. Then, out of the childlike innocence of the Cosmic Mother-Father/Goodness, we pass through the Holy Gates, for the password that allows us to cross over into life is innocence, the innocence of childlikeness.

We then carry innocence and goodness within us. We crystallize it as formalized thought, made from the speeding light of the universal intelligence of timelessness.

Timelessness changes into the slowed down light of crystallized linear time. The metaphor for time is the weaver's loom that weaves the tapestry that can now appear as life. Life looms forth into "breathing creativity that moves within highest effort." The experience of highest effort can be appreciated as life observes itself as the seedling working, sprouting, and then breaking the top layer of the cover soil of the Earth's infinite self. The Earth can, in seeking, find the spiritual, physical sunlight of its own being. We, the planting field of cosmic consciousness, become God's promise.

And so it was in the beginning, when the Great Farmer created a place for emergence. Then, in time, the energy of the vibrational landscape of cosmic thought had eyes to see and could see it's own radiance and beauty. Life had become the living manifesto of God's Beauty and then God came down to play. He made our clothes of playfulness so that we could wear them out of the resonance of his playful laughter. *Eh - piaah is* the vibration for playing. *Eh* means "God is here" and *piaah* means "making," and making would also mean that clothes, the cover of our physical body, would become the abode of God's flesh.

Silence

Even before time was, silence was, and silence had the attributes of *keee* (placement) - *aah* (purity) - *teh* (stop). Placement, purification, and stillness, or stopped-ness. *Keee ~ aah ~ neh* became mother. *Taah ~ me ~ ne* became father, and the sound of *teh* created the "Holding the Door Open," which created the present tense in consciousness. Placement was the primary essence vibration that became the mother, giver of life, so that now life could create. Purification was the primary essence that became the father, the purifier essence of placement. *Teh*, stopped-ness, gave them nowness or door-openness, as in the "here and now" of each moment, so that they could enter into all parallel realities — past, present, and future. First came placement, the mother, followed by the father, purity, and together they became the cosmic mother/father principle. They could be at all places past, present, and future simultaneously because of the presentness of Time.

I saw the weaver's loom as time weaving elaborate tapestries of the strands of God's discoveries among the heirlooms of memory.

Silence Is Broken

. . . and the silence was broken because the essence of get-up, *aah ~ wee ~ weh,* happened.

In the morning of daytimeness *kee ~ aah ~ teh* was awakened by *aah ~ wee ~ weh* (change), and now silence and non-silence began. Later vibration would allow us humans to appear and disappear from silence into other realms, randomly. And time became one part descending light, one part ascending light on which awareness, capacity to manifest, and relativity, were now allowables.

A Moment's Behavior

Since then, the nature of life reveals that every single moment is awakened from out of silence. The moment appears, then expresses its content, and returns back into silence. Every moment returns back into silence because its roots are there. Every moment is grounded in silence. And the roots in metaphor are what become the eternal flame of life. When a moment (insight in motion) makes its appearance on the stage of life, its content is purified by "*aah*" (breath), and the "*teh*" stops (to hold the door open) so that the moment can return back into silence.

And that is how silence (non-form place) can materialize, enjoy the movement of insight and the breath of placement — the essence of purity. It is the nature of silence to give placement to its life, to allow its own purification and then to stop the degree of its own expression. In metaphor silence is our physical blood in sound vibration, saying "yes" to life in accordance with our spiritual (breath) law as well as our natural (physical) law. Descending light is our spiritual law, whereas arising light is our natural law. We are Mother Nature's promise to herself.

Silence is made of three vibrations: I. placement; 2. purity; and 3. stillness. Another way of describing silence is that we know its home is in the Infinite Void. Technically it is the no-form place or the place of nothingness. Consequently, the true measure of our success in life is how much of, or the degree of nothingness (emptiness) we can achieve. There are three vibrations that came into existence after what I call the "*aah ~ wee ~ wah*" awakening moment: I. Now life could breathe; 2. now life could materialize; and 3. now life could move. Again, breath, materialization, and movement.

"Don't get stuck in the form" means don't get stuck in the breathing or in the materialization, or in the movements of life. Perhaps the most important thing to do is to return to silence, to become the finite and infinite of all knowingness. The idea I want to convey here is that we use the inner walls of our need to catch the revelations as they pass by us so that we can become states of illumination, so that we can become the shamanic journey of the observer and the observed in our everyday life experiences.

Walking as Vibration

Taah chee hu — walking — is the analogy for vibration. Every year during Holy Week I walk from Bernalillo, New Mexico to Chimayo, New Mexico, a distance of sixty-five miles, to honor the Santuario, the shrine to the Christ child. I do this because I understand that when we are physically walking, we become silence and non-silence inside of time. They are the spirit of the energies of walking which are in us.

In walking, when our foot impacts with the ground, the descending light marries ascending light in the sound of our feet on the earth, nourishing our whole bodies. The sound which starts at the foot travels then to all of the other body parts and shakes the old ways alive and implants the new. It is as if we have moved from "as above so below." This chant (nowness) sings of the energy which bonds the past, present, and future. This is sound energy, and it heals as it comes upon the energy that is lifting us awake. *Taah* — walkingness of the purifying father — gives us clarity of mind. *Chi* — alerts us to the "cold truth that knows," which then awakens the physical body for creative activity. *Hu* carries us next into the unknown.

Freedom from choice allows us to be crystallized images, and as crystals we can be our own seers, because we are Here and then disappear in order to be There. Just before we become the memory of the moment just gone by, we fall into the essence of awe. The flash of light is the illumination that takes us up beyond the darkness of the void, just before we materialize what we have experienced, just before we disappear once again into emptiness. The silence is our home while the being of time brings us momentarily out to weave us into an array of Beauty, just before we appear as silence.

Do we really exist? The answer I can give, having viewed all of the possibilities, is that, beyond the levels of our highest goodness, we are nothingness, working diligently for more of the same nothingness, so that we may be full. The true purpose of the practice of vibration is the self expression of the infinite in finiteness, because all of the One in the all is a sleeping, dreaming heart of Love.

The Purpose of Vibration

The active forms that make vibration a possibility include the *nature* of vibration, the *order* in which it happens, and the *revelation* aspect of it. The nature of vibration is that it has a quality of pulling in and pulling out. The order aspect of it flows toward emptiness, while the revelation side of it sees what is being made.

The first quality in the *nature* of vibration is that when it is pulling in, an increased heat level allows it to face its own nature. In pulling out, it nurtures its own nature.

Again, in the pulling in to its own nature, it faces what it is creating, while in the pulling out it nurtures that which it just allowed itself to become.

The *order* aspect of vibration gives it the sequence so that it can materialize a desired form. Apparently materialization occurs because vibration is seeking to purify the center (heart) of its newly formulated form. Consequently, the process of bringing forth gives it its materialization. Apparently, order also tends to move sequentially toward "lack of" or emptiness. It creates energy toward that end result by filling that space with a form.

Revelation, on the other hand, appears in the motion of energy, because the ability for the conscious awareness to see is created by movement. Without movement, it could not see what it was creating. Additionally, revelation is what creates the power to create even more forms. The nature, order, and revelation of energy gives continuity toward perpetuity because this is instilled in its very nature.

Finally, in true reality, we do not exist, and that innocence creates in us the capacity to seek ourselves in ourselves, to appear and disappear, so that we can have, moment by moment, a review of all we have cultivated. The Christos is our crystallization, our love for life.

*Joseph Rael and Mary Elizabeth Marlow can be contacted for further
information on any of the following:*

JOSEPH RAEL
P.O. Box 1309
Bernalillo, NM 87004
Book orders (*Beautiful Painted Arrow*)
Lectures, seminars and programs in the USA and Europe
Drum Dance
Tapes of Native American chants
Artwork & posters

MARY ELIZABETH MARLOW
903 Goldsboro Avenue
Virginia Beach, VA 23451
Book orders (*Handbook for the Emerging Woman*)
U.S. schedule
European schedule
Retreat programs
Joint programs with Joseph Rael
Lecture tapes